THE REAL READER'S QUARTERLY

# Slightly Foxed

'A Snatch of Morning'

D1385715

NO.58 SUMMER 2018

*Editors*  Gail Pirkis & Hazel Wood
*Marketing and publicity*  Stephanie Allen & Jennie Harrison Bunning
*Bookshops*  Anna Kirk
*Subscriptions*  Hattie Summers & Olivia Wilson

*Cover illustration by Debbie George*

Debbie George has been a painter for over twenty years. Her work is a celebration of her passion for flowers and the objects with which she surrounds herself. She finds inspiration in many forms, ranging from ceramics and plants to books and wallpaper, textiles and landscape. Assembling flowers or objects within the foreground of a painting and setting them against a variety of backdrops, Debbie builds up layers of paint that create a wonderful luminosity and depth. For more of her work see www.debbiegeorge.co.uk.

*Design by Octavius Murray*

*Layout by Andrew Evans*

*Colophon and tailpiece by David Eccles*

Published by Slightly Foxed Limited
53 Hoxton Square
London N1 6PB

tel  020 7033 0258
email  office@foxedquarterly.com
www.foxedquarterly.com

*Slightly Foxed* is published quarterly in early March, June, September and December

Annual subscription rates (4 issues)
UK and Ireland £40; Overseas £48

Single copies of this issue can be bought for £11 (UK) or £13 (Overseas)

All back issues in printed form are also available

ISBN 978-1-910898-18-5
ISSN 1742-5794

*Printed and bound by Smith Settle, Yeadon, West Yorkshire*

# Contents

## Contents

John Watson

For the digital edition of *Slightly Foxed* and an up-to-date list of partners
and membership benefits, please visit the members' page on our website:
www.foxedquarterly.com/members or contact Olivia:
olivia@foxedquarterly.com · +44 (0) 20 7033 0258

The Slightly Foxed office can obtain all books reviewed in this issue,
whether new or second-hand. Please contact Anna:
anna@foxedquarterly.com · +44 (0) 20 7033 0258

# From the Editors

For some months now the office in Hoxton Square has been ringing to the sounds of hammering, banging, drilling, and tools dropping on to scaffolding, and we've often struggled to hear one another speak. If you build an extension in London today it can usually only go up or down, and our freeholder is adding an extra couple of storeys. We're told the agony is nearly over and now it's summer we're looking forward to coming out of forced hibernation and opening the windows.

Nevertheless it's been business as usual at Slightly Foxed. Jennie is continuing to develop the website, which is also gradually serving more and more as an *SF* community noticeboard where we post information we think will be of interest to subscribers and where eventually, we hope, subscribers can communicate with one another and with us. We're gradually extending our range of membership benefits too, setting up partnerships with independent bookshops and institutions such as the London Library and the Royal Society of Literature to offer subscribers special terms. If you have any suggestions for possible new partners, do please get in touch.

The Slightly Foxed Writers' Competition produced a record number of entries this year, all of them worth reading. Subjects tackled were many and various, from Dr Johnson to taxidermy, and we had such difficulty choosing a winner that we finally opted to award a joint first prize. The two pieces we chose are very different, but both are examples of how books can change a life. One is Alastair Glegg's account of being introduced to books at his prep school, where the masters instilled in him a love of words and encouraged him to become a real reader. It is affectionate and evocative, and led us to think of the difference between his experience and that of a child who is taught mechanically to decipher words on a page but is given no feel for the magic of reading – a lesson for our test-obsessed government. The other was Richard Crockatt's elegant and thoughtful piece on the galvanizing effect of studying Thomas Mann's *The Magic Mountain* at a particular moment in history and in his own life. Congratulations to them both. They will each receive £250 and we look forward to publishing their pieces. Three others were also, we felt, worthy of publication and so as runners-up Janet Walkinshaw, Posy Fallowfield and Peter Radford will each receive £100 and see their pieces in *SF* in due course. Our thanks to everyone who entered.

And finally to our summer Slightly Foxed Edition, *The Blue Field* (see p.14), which completes John Moore's trilogy based in and around his home town of Tewkesbury, lightly disguised as Elmbury in the books, and the village of Brensham. Between them they take the reader from the end of the First World War, when a country town like Tewkesbury had a sturdy independent life of its own, to the aftermath of the Second, when in Brensham the heavy hand of the War Agricultural Executive Committee is being felt and the developers and weekenders have started to arrive. The hero of *The Blue Field* is farmer William Hart, a man who refuses to be cowed by the authorities, and his story is both touching and hilarious. A must for anyone who has already enjoyed *Portrait of Elmbury* and *Brensham Village* (see SFEs nos. 26 and 34) and a pleasure in store for any lover of the rural past who hasn't. And as you may notice if you order, we've taken another small ecological step by doing away with bubble wrap and substituting a wrapping of corrugated cardboard!

GAIL PIRKIS & HAZEL WOOD

# A Snatch of Morning

HELEN MACEWAN

I bought David Cecil's Life of William Cowper, *The Stricken Deer*, at a time, in my early twenties, when I was starting to devour literary biography, my preferred reading ever since. I was by then familiar not just with Elizabeth Bennet and Jane Eyre and David Copperfield but with Jane Austen, the Brontës and Charles Dickens. Most of my literary friends were in the nineteenth century: the eighteenth was largely unfamiliar territory. All I knew about William Cowper was that he had been a favourite poet of Jane Austen's.

It was David Cecil who changed that. At the time I knew no more about Cecil than I did about Cowper, but over the years, as his books lined up on my shelves, he too became a literary friend. A willowy figure who grew up in the Cecils' ancestral home, Hatfield House, and married into the Bloomsbury group, he started out as a historian before becoming an Oxford literature don. *The Stricken Deer* was his first book, published in 1929 when he was only 27.

For Cecil, an unacademic academic who had little time for doctrine, reading literature was all about enjoyment, and teaching it was about transmitting that enjoyment. The imagination excited him more than scholarship, people more than theories. F. R. Leavis frowned on him as a dilettante, but students fondly recalled his breathless enthusiasm and the magical flow of his conversation.

---

David Cecil, *The Stricken Deer, or the Life of William Cowper* (1929)
Faber Finds · Pb · 316pp · £16 · ISBN 9780571251643
William Cowper is also the subject of Alexandra Harris's piece in Issue 53 about the pleasures of reading Cowper's letters, 'The Abyss Beyond the Orchard'.

It is surprising to learn from his friend L. P. Hartley that Cecil, an inveterate talker, found writing, by contrast, hard labour. On a train to Venice while he was writing *The Stricken Deer*, he kept his sleeping-car companion awake with his groans as he worked on the manuscript through the night, but by morning he had produced just three sentences. The lyrical flow of his prose gives no sense of the effort that went into it.

'From the first the atmosphere in which Cowper passed his life was domestic.' Like the opening of a novel by Jane Austen, a writer Cecil greatly admired, that first sentence, containing the key words 'atmosphere' – all-important in a Cecil biography – and 'domestic' – the sphere in which he most loved to observe his subjects – pulls us straight into Cowper's life.

The cosy contentedness of Cowper's early childhood in a Hertfordshire village was short-lived. His mother's death when he was only 6 left him ill-equipped for life beyond Great Berkhamsted rectory, and this, and the bullying he encountered at his first school, must have contributed to the depression that dogged him thereafter. Timid and affectionate, he did not regain the stable domestic background so necessary to him until years later. Meanwhile he was happier at a second school, Westminster, and then learning law with a London solicitor, Mr Chapman, in Ely Place. He took little interest in his law studies but enjoyed the company of his fellow trainee:

Easy-going Mr Chapman did not bother them much; and they used to sit for hours, two excited boys in the formal dress of 1752, discussing books and people . . . and going off into fits of laughter and then growing very serious again, while the evening sky darkened to night behind the worn traceries of St Etheldreda's, and the bending trees in its churchyard.

Cecil somehow succeeds in condensing the atmosphere of a whole epoch of Cowper's life into a single sentence.

Despite congenial male companions, what Cowper yearned for was family life and female company. These were provided on visits to a family of cousins, one of whom, Theodora, was his first love. When her father forbade their marriage and Cowper found himself, a brief-less barrister, in dingy lodgings in the Temple, depression soon set in. The prospect of a *viva voce* examination for a clerkship in the House of Lords proved too much for his fragile mental state and precipi-tated the first of several periods of insanity.

'There is in the human spirit', writes Cecil, 'an upward thrust of vitality that can only be defeated by death. Torn up by the roots, trodden underfoot . . . the soul will yet, after a little time, again revive . . . Cowper's spirit, so fragile, so bruised, so resilient, once more began to climb from the abyss into which it had fallen.' When he finally emerged, it was as a convert to Evangelicalism and in a state of exaltation that kept him buoyed up for some years.

Unfortunate as Cowper was in some ways, his life was equally remarkable for its strokes of luck. Now 33, he had no sooner left Dr Cotton's lunatic asylum for solitary lodgings in Huntingdon than he met a young clergyman called William Unwin who invited him to tea to meet his parents. The father, also a clergyman, was elderly, the mother, Mary, much younger. It was to her that Cowper became closest. He had found the family he needed. He moved in as a lodger with this quiet Evangelical household.

On Mr Unwin's death the remaining household moved to Olney to sit at the feet of an Evangelical clergyman with a chequered past called John Newton. Cowper was safe from depression as long as he was caught up in the whirl of Newton's activities. But as his faith waned, a second spell of madness closed in, ten years after the first. It took the form of religious mania, a conviction that he was sentenced to eternal damnation. Thanks to Mary Unwin's devoted care he recov-ered his sanity but not his religious fervour. He was now convinced, even when sane, that he was damned in the next life, but he resolved to enjoy this one, in a quiet way, as well as he could.

Howard Phipps, 'The Medlar Tree', wood engraving

Cowper and Mary Unwin had become indispensable to one another. A plan to marry came to nothing – the imminent prospect of matrimony threw Cowper into panic – but they continued, platonically, to share a home. He needed support and companionship, she someone to whom she could devote herself. In Orchard Side, their poky house on Olney High Street near Newton's church, Cowper kept the forces of darkness at bay by constant occupation. At first this took the form of gardening and caring for a menagerie of pets, including his tame hares Bess, Puss and Tiny. Cecil is at his most vivid when evoking the scenes of domestic content so often described by Cowper himself. His favourite time of day was tea-time, particularly on winter afternoons when the candles were lit, the curtains drawn against approaching night and the kettle boiled for 'the cup that cheers but not inebriates'.

The rain might drum on the window [Cecil writes], the wind whistle along the deserted street; it only emphasized the warmth and comfort inside, where the kettle hummed, and the cat lapped up its milk, and Cowper and Mary laughed over the day's happenings. They were interrupted by the twang of a horn and the hollow sound of the galloping of hoofs outside. It was the post arriving at the Bull Inn.

The letters and newspapers from London were brought in, to be read aloud by Cowper to Mary while she darned his stockings.

To this placid round was added versifying, which he took up as a diversion at the age of 49, often writing in his greenhouse in the garden. He became a poet of domesticity – starting the first book of his very long poem *The Task* with the words 'I sing the sofa' – and of the natural world, painting in verse the Buckinghamshire country-side around Olney where he and Mary took their walks. It was a landscape as tame as that of Hertfordshire. Even the Wilderness, a spot Cowper loved, was a tame wilderness, a creation of Capability Brown's in Weston Park, the property of the local squire Mr Throckmorton.

With the success of *The Task* Cowper found himself sought after, and his social circle expanded. Cecil tells us that Newton, as Cowper's spiritual mentor, was concerned he was becoming less serious-minded. Cowper sought to allay his fears: 'Newton need not worry. He was still fundamentally miserable, and Mrs Unwin still spent hours pray-ing for him.' However, Newton was not wholly reassured. 'He had heard for a fact that Cowper had been seen in a green coat and had even taken part in an archery competition . . . '

At the invitation of the Throckmortons, Cowper and Mary moved to more attractive accommodation in nearby Weston Lodge. The Throckmortons were ideal neighbours, and Weston Underwood, Cecil tells us in one of his most lyrical passages, was 'the perfect English village of idyllic imagination, where red-coated huntsmen jingle gallantly to the Meet on a soft autumn morning, or, on a glow-ing evening in summer the cumbrous hay-carts creak home with sun-bonneted children perched atop'.

But the fragility of Cowper's mental health meant that the idyll could not last. There were always two Cowpers. However happy his sane, daytime life, his nights were often a frightful tussle with his demons. In fearful dreams he would hear from God's own lips that he was doomed. The death of Mary's son William and the breakdown of her health, resulting from a series of strokes, brought on new attacks of depression and madness. Yet this period produced one of his most touching poems:

> . . . still to love, though prest with ill,
> In wintry age to feel no chill,
> With me is to be lovely still,
>     My Mary!

The account of the pair's last years is almost unbearably sad, and the devotion of the relatives who stepped in when Cowper could no longer cope almost unbearably moving. A further stroke changed Mary's personality, transforming the calm presence who had been the rock of Cowper's life into a querulous tyrant prone to persecution mania. Not surprisingly, his sanity shattered under the strain. They both died far from Olney in the house of a young cousin who cared for them in their final decline, Cowper, on his deathbed, unshaken in his expectation of eternal damnation.

His poem of despair 'The Castaway' is perhaps his greatest, but the bulk of his poetry is that of the gentle, humorous Cowper who kept himself sane by writing about the small happenings of his life – the felling of a much-loved poplar grove, the death of a pet hare.

In his introduction, Cecil speaks of the difficulty of understanding a past era in all its complexity. Each age, he says, tends to recreate past ones in 'the image of its own desire'. Did he heed this warning himself? The Olney world he paints in *The Stricken Deer* is an idyllic one that could be summed up by his sketch of life in the Unwin household: 'There was a snatch of morning about it, a nursery freshness, an inno-cent, lavender-scented sweetness.' The sense of an idyll is enhanced by the beauty of his prose. Yet his account of Cowper's world is substan-tiated by Cowper's own descriptions in poems and letters.

Cecil does, however, give us a brief glimpse of a very different eighteenth-century world. His account of John Newton's life before his conversion to Evangelicalism seems to belong to another, darker, book: his early years at sea with his merchant-seaman father, then later being press-ganged into the Royal Navy, a spell working in virtual slavery on an African plantation and involvement in the actual slave trade as captain of a slave ship. Cowper wrote anti-slavery poems, and a biographer of our own post-colonial age would make more of this theme.

But David Cecil was in his element writing about quiet lives. A subsequent study – of Dorothy Osborne and Thomas Grey – is called just that, *Two Quiet Lives*. His biography of Charles Lamb is the story of a placid life broken, like Cowper's, by recurring madness (that of Charles's sister Mary); Charles and Mary Lamb were another odd, devoted couple, like Cowper and Mary Unwin.

I opened *The Stricken Deer* knowing Cowper only as a vague figure in a wig, as in the frontispiece of my edition, or sometimes in an odd turban – someone who belonged to an age I thought I didn't know. By the time I closed it William Cowper was a friend, and the eighteenth century was no longer unknown territory but recognizable (at least Cowper's bit of it) as the world Jane Austen's novels came from. More than that, the book planted a seed. When, much later, I started to write in earnest, I knew I wanted to write literary biographies.

I have read a lot of them since. Many have been more densely packed with information; most, unlike *The Stricken Deer*, have been equipped with indexes and annotations. But few biographical subjects have entered my imagination as completely as David Cecil's gentle, tormented William Cowper.

HELEN MACEWAN is a translator and former teacher. In her free time she enjoys organizing literary events and writing. She is the author of books about Charlotte Brontë's time in Brussels, which has been her home for the past decade, and of a life of Winifred Gérin, a Brontë biographer with a Belgian link.

# Sprouts and Parsnip Wine

SARAH PERRY

Early one morning, late in July, the villagers of 'crack-brained Brensham' woke to a remarkable spectacle. There amid the customary colours of furze and wheat was a seven-acre field that 'had suddenly become tinctured with the colour of Mediterranean skies'. Nothing like it had ever happened before, so that the villagers caught their breath at the sight of this miracle: a great, vivid patch of cerulean 'so clear and pure that it made one think of eyes or skies'.

There could be no doubt who was responsible for this act of rebellion: William Hart, who – against the directives of government authorities, and in defiance of the farmer's ordinary seasonal rotations – had planted a field of linseed. '"Have you seen old William's field?" people said. "It does your heart good to look at it; but Lord, I wouldn't be in his shoes when the trouble starts!"'

*The Blue Field* is the last in John Moore's trilogy which pays tribute to an England that seems, somehow, both absolutely familiar and impossibly remote. I first encountered Brensham during an arduous recovery from illness. A lifelong walker and seeker-out of hidden places, I was unable to wander much more than ten minutes from home, but to read John Moore was to be transported instantly away from the dreariness of recuperation to a fragrant field in high summer.

If the first two books of the trilogy are portraits of places – Elmbury, a proxy for Tewkesbury, Moore's birthplace; and Brensham, an amalgam of nearby villages (see *SF* nos. 42 and 50) – *The Blue Field* is largely a portrait of a man:

I am going to tell you the story of a man of Brensham who was so wild and intractable and turbulent that he failed, in the end, to come to terms with our orderly world (or perhaps one could say that our orderly world had failed to come to terms with him).

This wild, intractable, turbulent man is William Hart, farmer of the blue field: descendant, so he insists, of Shakespeare himself; vast as an oak; hot-tempered and gentle; a roisterer, brawler and tamer of foxes; sower of wild oats across the county, and possessed of a genius for

Anne Hayward, wood engraving

contriving strong drink out of everything from a parsnip to a pea pod. Hart, we suspect, did not exist – or at any rate, not quite: Moore frankly confessed to 'playing fast-and-loose with chronology and topography', and preserved the privacy of his subjects by changing their names. And yet the reader is left with little doubt that here is a portrait as accurate and acute as if captured by digital camera, not merely of a man, but of a kind of Englishness.

The reader follows Hart through his boisterous, untamed youth, which is all love affairs and brawls; through various stand-offs with the authorities and with those who would consider themselves his betters; to Moore's last glimpse of him, his face 'brown as shoe leather and wrinkled as a russet apple in the New Year'. Moore's prose is so lively, and he is so attentive to dialect and foible, that William Hart erupts into the room as the pages are turned, trailing in his wake the scent of bee orchids and beer, and the sound of Land Girls preparing for an evening's dance.

Moore was a pioneer conservationist, but his subject here is not this ancient hedgerow or that threatened garden bird, but rather the human animal and its habitat. Incidents in Hart's life – reported with Moore's distinctive, stylish blend of erudition, wit and bosky atmosphere – are attended by a vivid and varied cast in the tradition of Eliot, Dickens and Shakespeare. There is Mr Chorlton, the retired schoolmaster, and his friend Sir Gerald, who came home from a Japanese prisoner-of-war camp wizened in body, but not in spirit; there are the rascally Bardolph, Pistol and Nym, who behave in every respect like their Shakespearean namesakes; there is Mrs Halliday, wife of the Labour MP, a 'very intelligent young woman' who understands instinctively that she will fit 'into the jigsaw-puzzle' of Brensham's little world.

The desultory reader may perhaps consider Moore a sentimentalist (after all, he referred to his own novels as 'country contentments'). But there is something clear-eyed and direct in his portrait of Brensham which recalls John Berger's portrait of a country doctor, *A Fortunate Man*. It is, above all, an act of witness, though Moore speaks from within the village: he writes not of 'them', but of 'us', and can recognize a sprout-picker at twenty paces by the shape of their bottom as they stoop over the frozen fields.

*The Blue Field* was published in 1948, and marks a liminal time between war's aftermath and the coming of modernity. Here are farmer's boys who 'flew as tail-gunners through the fiery night above Berlin', and here is George Daniels, who has not taken off his paratrooper's jacket since he landed in Normandy on D-Day (Moore himself was present at D-Day as a press attaché, and one can't help but wonder if he, too, clung on to some sartorial remnant of the war). But here also is the Syndicate, a sinister collection of would-be developers, entrepreneurs and out-of-towners, taking over the moth-eaten home of the local squire; here is a Labour MP, newly installed with his visionary wife, forever raising questions in Parliament as to the villagers' habits of sanitation, parenting and farm husbandry. What Moore brings to Brensham is nothing so saccharine as sentiment, but rather a fond compassionate gaze. When he writes, as he does often and with a kind wit, of soft-eyed Pru Hart, 'the naughtiest girl in Brensham', who cannot be kept indoors at night, but rather wanders the fields at dusk seeking out lovers (in due course doing so with prams full of her offspring), he does so without either judgement or prurient glee. He seems to say: we have always been like this, and always shall be, and there is nothing wrong with that.

If the book is in some respects a museum piece, it has by no means gathered dust. Now and then something startles the reader in its immediacy and contemporaneity, such as William's horror at the local fox hunt, in which he seems not some smocked yokel in a Constable painting, but a progressive who would sit well among twenty-first-century hunt saboteurs, so long as strong beer was supplied. When Moore turns his pen to the local gypsies, who have forsaken their ancestors' wandering ways and taken up residence on the outskirts of Brensham, the reader may prepare an anticipatory wince at any forthcoming infelicities with regard to minorities, but Moore writes of them with precisely the same benevolent amusement with which he writes of the English farm boys or their sprout-picking paramours:

Life has always been hard for them, and now that our own high standard of living is dwindling fast, and the cold winds of the world are blowing one by one our precious amenities away, they might laugh at our discomfiture and our grumbling – if they ever troubled themselves enough about our affairs to be amused by them.

Indeed, the reader may be struck by how Brensham embraces the Polish Count Pniack, who marries a local girl and is forever trying to explain the pronunciation of his name ('The P is silent!'); and by how the gypsies represent, for Moore, qualities of English life which are threatened by the first inklings of globalization ('I don't mind betting that their hens will still be scratching about under their caravans when our last dollar has bought the last packet of dried eggs from America!'). The villains of the book are interlopers not on national grounds, but on ideological ones – not least the Syndicate:

> The village passionately hated them, and there was an element of fear in the hatred, for it really looked at one time as if the Syndicate would overwhelm Brensham and impose their shabby get-rich-quick regime upon it, tyrannize and subdue and cheapen and emasculate it, and turn it at last into a tributary province of their far-flung financial empire.

What it is to be English has always been a contentious and largely unanswerable question, demanding reference to so many contributing cultures that one thinks instinctively of Daniel Defoe's line that the English are 'a mongrel race'. To read *The Blue Field* is to see everything about Englishness that is universal and common – a Brensham lad wrote home during the war: 'The [French] are very good farmers. They drink cider. If they didn't speak Frog they'd be just like us. It makes you think.' – but also to recognize, with a kind of nostalgic calling on half-forgotten memory, an Englishness that cannot easily be weaponized to malign political effect. It is the Englishness of parsnip wine drunk in imprudent quantities, and of devoting time to the cultivation and the eating of sprouts; of grudges nursed in unspoken silence, until the matter can only be settled with fists; of diffident offers of friendship, and of lust in the fields in midsummer, when there's little else to be getting on with; of squires in pink coats bawling at truculent villagers who favour foxes above the aristocracy, and impecunious lords giving their last shilling to young mothers while the roof of their stately home rots about their noble ears. Perhaps most of all, it is the very particular Englishness of rebelling – in however small, petty or impotent a fashion – against rules and regulations impinging on individual liberty, even 'when the trouble starts'; of a single field of linseed in full bloom, flown like a blue silk flag at the foot of Brensham Hill.

SARAH PERRY is the author of *The Essex Serpent*, and is fond of parsnip wine. Her second novel, *Melmoth*, will be published in October.

---

The final volume in John Moore's trilogy, *The Blue Field* (256pp), is now available in a limited and numbered cloth-bound edition of 2,000 copies (subscriber price: UK & Eire £16, Overseas £18; non-subscriber price: UK & Eire £17.50, Overseas £19.50). All prices include post and packing. Copies may be ordered by post (53 Hoxton Square, London N1 6PB), by phone (020 7033 0258) or via our website www.foxedquarterly.com.

Copies of the first two volumes in the trilogy, *Portrait of Elmbury* and *Brensham Village*, are also still available as Slightly Foxed Editions.

# *The Price of Power*

PATRICK WELLAND

An American academic in charge of creative writing at the University of Denver writes three novels in twelve years. They are unconnected apart from a shared fastidious composition. The first (1960) is set in Kansas in the 1870s and concerns a young man looking for adventure in the wilderness of the West. The second (1965) traces the unexceptional life of an assistant professor at a Midwestern university in the first half of the last century. Little more than a ripple of appreciation is raised. In contrast, the third novel (1972) – an account of Rome's first emperor, Augustus – shares the US National Book Award for Fiction. Yet it is a brief efflorescence. Soon the book is interred with its predecessors in that well-stocked necropolis of forgotten literary talent. The author dies twenty-two years later, in 1994, a further novel unfinished at the time of his death.

The three books were *Butcher's Crossing*, *Stoner* and *Augustus*, their author the peppery, chain-smoking John Williams – and there it might have ended. But in the early 2000s resurrection stirred. Through a grapevine of still appreciative readers and booksellers, interest reawakened in *Stoner* with its meticulous dissection of love, conflict and loss. The book was reissued and, after a hesitant start, sales took off. In 2013, the forty-one-year-old novel was voted Best Book of the Year by Waterstones.

It was only after reading *Stoner* that I looked at the brief list of Williams's previous works (they include a fourth novel – his first,

John Williams, *Augustus* (1972)
Vintage · Pb · 352pp · £9.99 · ISBN 9780099445081

written in 1948 – which he later disowned). The title *Augustus* immediately attracted me. Direct me to novels about the classical world
and I am as a white bull with gilded horns to the slaughter. It has
been so ever since I read an easily digestible version of the *Odyssey* as
a child. Could this match Marguerite Yourcenar's Hadrian (*SF* no. 2),
Robert Graves's Claudius, Mary Renault's Alexander and Theseus,
and Henry Treece's Oedipus, Jason and Electra? Yes.

The outline of Augustus's life is well known although contemporary sources are exiguous. Born Gaius Octavius in 63 BC into a
wealthy equestrian family, he was the maternal great-nephew of
Caesar and at the age of 17 was adopted by the dictator and made his
heir. Thereafter, he was known as Octavian. After Caesar was murdered in 44 BC, the young man moved with fellow triumvirs Mark
Antony and Marcus Lepidus to crush his adoptive father's assassins.
In the continuing fallout from the collapse of the Republic, the triumvirate fell apart, with Octavian emerging master in 31 BC after
defeating Antony at the naval battle of Actium.

The civil war over, he set about cementing his power and settling
Rome's empire through conquest and diplomacy. In doing so,
Octavian laid down the ideological and institutional framework
which would sustain that empire for the next 400 years. He died
aged 76 in AD 14 having been granted the honorific title of Augustus
('one to be revered') and worshipped in his lifetime as a living god,
an elevation by the credulous that he considered absurd.

Throughout, this wily manipulator insisted he was but a servant
of the people, uninterested in retaining power should they wish
otherwise. This disingenuous fiction fooled no one. Tacitus says in
his *Annals*: 'He seduced the army with bonuses and the citizenry with
corn – and everyone with the sweetness of peace. Then he took to
himself the functions of the Senate, the magistrates and the laws.
There was no opposition . . .' Gibbon more bluntly described
Augustus's rule as an 'absolute monarchy disguised by the forms of a
commonwealth'.

So how does an author who so precisely unpicked the narrow life of a professor at a twentieth-century university handle the dramatic canvas presented by Rome's greatest emperor 2,000 years earlier?

Above all, Williams's primary intention was authenticity. Anxious to avoid the clichés attached to the Roman empire – murderous toga-plotting, dodgy sex, heroic gladiators and swivel-eyed barbarians erupting from dank Teutonic forests – he said:

I didn't think I could handle it in a straight narrative style without making it sound like a Cecil B. DeMille movie or a historical romance. I wanted the characters to present themselves. These people were very real and contemporaneous to me. I didn't want to try to explain them.

To achieve this subjective realism, the book takes the epistolary form of a series of letters, memoirs, documents and dispatches written by friends, family and enemies over the course of Octavian's struggle for supremacy. As the awkward teenager matures into avenger, then lawmaker and finally 'father' of his people, these observers mark his passage with praise, fear, criticism and admiration.

This illustration of the truth that an individual's actions can be perceived differently by different people is complemented by Williams's portrayal of Octavian as protean. He instinctively senses it is his destiny to change the world. For this to be achieved, he must change himself – to 'find or invent within himself some hard and secret part that is indifferent to himself, to others and even to the world he is destined to remake'. As death nears, the old emperor admits that 'like any poor, pitiable shell of an actor' he has played so many parts there no longer is 'himself'.

*Augustus* comprises three books. Book I traces Octavian's rise to power from the moment that he learns at 19 of Caesar's murder. His youthful friend, the louche Maecenas, recalls him then stricken by grief, 'a pleasant stripling, no more, with a face too delicate to receive the blows of fate, with a manner too diffident to achieve purpose'. But another early supporter, Agrippa, senses the underlying steel. Octavian relies on Agrippa's military expertise at the crucial battles of Mutina, Philippi (at which some historians have suspected him of cowardice), Naulochus and Actium. Unlike gossipy Maecenas, Agrippa recalls those turbulent days in straightforward, almost clipped, language, reflecting his character as a no-nonsense soldier not given to flights of literary fancy.

Cicero, pious citadel of Republican virtue, is contemptuous of the young upstart. He tells his correspondent Marcius Philippus after the Ides assassination: 'He is a boy and a rather foolish boy at that; he has no idea of politics nor is he likely to have . . . thus he does not, I believe, constitute a danger for us.' Foolish Cicero. He will be murdered in the triumvirate's Proscriptions. Antony, too, is patronizing. That boozy old dog of war writes to Octavian as seasoned hand to impetuous tyro. Leave it to me, son. Then the tone changes to exasperation, even panic, as he realizes he is being outmanoeuvred by that 'bloody hypocrite'. Foolish Antony. He will commit suicide after Actium.

These recollections and memoirs are interspersed with evocative descriptions of Rome and Alexandria, military commands, reports of senatorial proceedings, petitions and memoranda plus further correspondence from, among others, Livy, Horace, the historian Nicolaus of Damascus and the geographer Strabo of Amasia. In the process, Octavian's character is not so much unpeeled as layered with successive skins of ambiguity.

Book II moves largely from public to private life which, through necessity, Octavian has sacrificed to his perception of the general good. It includes the memoirs of the emperor's sexually charged daughter Julia, whom he unwillingly exiles for breaking his own law on adultery and thereby threatening the moral legitimacy of the ruling family. John McGahern tells us in an introduction that it was Williams's fascination with this story, first heard from the writer Morton Hunt, that led him to write the novel.

At the time of writing Julia is 43, condemned to the barren isle of Pandateria with only her crabby mother and a servant for company. But in her youthful pomp she was, through marriage to Agrippa and the adoption of her sons by Octavian, second only to the emperor's wife Livia. Although she has power, she cannot seize it like a man by force of strength. So, like her father, she conceives identities to disguise her desire for glory and works them to her advantage: innocent daughter, virtuous wife, imperious matron. Forced after Agrippa's death to marry Tiberius, Livia's unappealing son by her first marriage and the next emperor, she abandons caution and adopts her final role of adulterous libertine. Foolish Julia. Her last lover is linked to a plot against Octavian. She must go. Yet her father's love for her is undimmed.

To close, in Book III we hear the voice of the dying Augustus as he sails to Capri, teeth gone, hands trembling with palsy and drooping flesh blotched with age. We have witnessed through others his rise to power, his harshness and leniency, bravery and caution, his constant dissimulation. Now Augustus explains the paradox of that power – that his greatest strength is the recognition of his own weakness. Knowledge of it enables him successfully to exploit the weakness of others.

Looking back on his life with unsparing honesty, the *princeps* discloses that when Caesar was killed, far from being consumed by grief – as Maecenas believed – he 'felt nothing'. Then he was secretly overcome by elation. 'It was destiny that seized me that afternoon nearly sixty years ago, and I chose not to avoid its embrace.'

The terrible cost of that destiny, however, is abandonment of human relationships for, he says, it was never politic to let another know his heart. That denial of what is cherished includes losing the affection of his proud and arrogant wife who supported him to the end. Their love, eroded by Livia's ambition for her son, was short-lived. Yet Augustus appreciates her understanding of power and the sacrifices that have to be made for the sake of order. It has been plausibly suggested that Livia killed her ailing husband with poisoned figs. If so, he would have approved, for she would have done so to ensure the smooth dynastic succession of her son.

As the shades fall, the old man acknowledges his legacy, but he knows it is transitory. Rome will fall, the barbarian will conquer. None of it matters. 'The winds and rains of time will at last crumble the most solid stone, and there is no wall that can be built to protect the human heart from its own weakness.' It is said that among his last words were 'Have I played my part in the farce of life well enough?'

PATRICK WELLAND is a freelance writer. The closest he has come to the imperial purple is in some of his more excitable prose from his days as a Fleet Street sub-editor.

# Travelling Fearlessly

MAGGIE FERGUSSON

In 1992, I started working for a strange but beguiling organization. The Royal Society of Literature was, in those days, housed in a huge, dilapidated mansion in Bayswater, and it was there that its Fellows gathered to raise a farewell glass to my predecessor. They were an elderly, rather moth-eaten bunch, but one stood out – a strikingly handsome younger man in a velvet jacket. Somebody introduced me: 'This is Colin Thubron. He'll be a great support to you.'

And so he proved – when he was in London. For great tracts of time he was away, leaving his 'old self behind', exploring places most of us would neither dare nor desire to visit, but which we love to read about with a vicarious sense of fearlessness and endurance. In the golden generation that produced Jonathan Raban, Bruce Chatwin, Paul Theroux and Redmond O'Hanlon, Thubron is now the Grand Old Man, bringing to journeys that are physically and psychologically testing a fine, romantic sensibility. Even when there is apparently nothing to describe, his prose is seductively beautiful: 'A traveller needs to believe in the significance of where he is, and therefore in his own meaning,' he writes in *In Siberia* (1999), as he chugs by train towards the Arctic Circle. 'But now the earth is flattening out over its axis. The shoreline is sinking away. Nothing, it seems, has ever happened here.'

We meet on an autumn morning, sun streaming through the

---

Colin Thubron's travel books *Mirror to Damascus* (1967), *Among the Russians* (1983) and *Behind the Wall* (1987) are all available as Vintage paperbacks at £9.99 each. *In Siberia* (1999) is out of print but we can obtain second-hand copies.

French windows of Thubron's elegant Holland Park drawing-room. We sit in deep, white sofas, eating biscuits. Surely Thubron, now 79, can't want to leave all this behind and subject himself to the challenges and privations of another three-month journey? Yes, he says. He does. He is preparing himself to travel down the Amur, the ninth longest river in the world. It runs between Russia and China, so he is brushing up the Russian and Mandarin he learned for *Among the Russians* (1983) and *Behind the Wall* (1987). He is also playing regular games of tennis with his Russian tutor, to keep fit – 'although I've been rather lucky on that score: I've been fit all my life'.

One might expect him also to be building up lists of contacts – people to track down and interview when he arrives. But no. 'What I'm looking for, when I travel, is people in their context. In China, for example, I don't want somebody giving me information about the Cultural Revolution, I want somebody to tell me what they suffered in it. The people I'm speaking to are mainly working-class, they're farmers or petit bourgeoisie. Meeting them depends on serendipity, and I like that.'

It also depends on Thubron planting himself in some pretty grim places – fifth-class railway carriages stinking of sweat and urine, aisles awash with cigarette ash and phlegm; rat-infested hotels; cafés serving stomach-churning food. Travelling through China, he often had no idea where the next meal was coming from. And when an opportunity to eat presented itself, a menu might read like this: 'Steamed Cat, Braised Guinea Pig (whole) with Mashed Shrimps, Grainy Dog Meat with Chilli and Scallion in Soya Sauce, Shredded Cat Thick Soup, Fried Grainy Mud Puppy . . . Braised Python'. In Siberia, of all the meals he describes, the most palatable is 'pony in a cream mushroom sauce'.

As he travels, weight drops off him, he becomes physically depleted, he comes close to breaking-point. But he has never been tempted to give up. 'I don't tend to be worried on a physical level – and in a way the more extreme things become, the more exciting they are.' In fact, he feels a duty to his readers to expose himself to danger. During his 6,000-mile journey through Siberia, he made a spur-of-the-moment decision to climb aboard a 'damn great cargo boat' and ask to be dropped off at the remote, benighted village of Potalovo. He was warned against it: its Entsy inhabitants were, almost to a man, ne'er-do-wells and drunks, frequently violent. The only sympathetic character Thubron met was a doctor, marooned Ben Gunn-like in this bleak outpost, and sustained by just two books: a pocket edition of Kipling's poems and *A Thousand English Jokes*. Nobody could say when the next tanker might pass by to return Thubron to relative civilization. He could have been there for months.

> You do these things that are perhaps a little extreme, like stopping off at Potalovo (people said, 'Don't! You'll be knifed!') and you think, 'Should I, or shouldn't I?' The first thought is, 'I don't want to be knifed.' But the second is what good copy it will provide. And the third is that if you don't do it, you are letting down your book, and letting down the culture. You're refusing to see an integral and important part of the country you're travelling in. You've lapsed in your responsibility. So often the things you are hesitant to do yield something really good.

Certainly the pages on Potalovo in *In Siberia* make for grimly compulsive reading.

In recent months, Thubron's time has been taken up with reading scores of novels as a judge for the Man Booker Prize. But now that this is over, and he can devote himself to reading up about the Amur, he is longing to be off. 'The more I research, the more I'm itching to go. The more I can see the shape of the journey, the more excited I get.' But as he gears up there are two things that cause him apprehension. 'I do worry about bureaucracy, the police, oppression from above rather than chaos from below.'

In the Soviet Union, in the 1980s, he was followed by the KGB who confiscated all his notes (his writing looks as if an army of tiny ants, dipped in ink, has danced all over the pages: the KGB, baffled, gave him the benefit of the doubt and handed them back). Amur is a 'political river'. He fears it might get nasty again. And then he fears 'sterility' – not finding people who will talk to him. Over the years, he has developed techniques to combat this. He seeks out places where people won't easily be able to escape him. In China, for example, he followed a man into a public bath house, and stripped off all his clothes: 'I had an idea that the stripping off of clothes might strip away mental barriers too.' One by one, naked Chinese men began to speak to him.

Often, though he knows what he wants to find out from someone, instinct tells him that to ask direct questions won't work. 'So one thing I do is to expose myself a bit too. Then it's as if you're both going downhill, and you're preceding them in giving yourself away. You tell them you too have a terrible time with your income, or you've had a row with your wife. You let them feel it's OK to expose themselves on that level.' Crucial to this is the fact that Thubron is always travelling alone: 'If you're on your own, you're the oddity, and you are forced into understanding other people. I like to think I'm transparent. Of course I'm not. I carry my culture around like a pilgrim's sin on my back . . .'

Hand in hand with these ploys goes exceptional charm. Thubron is not just handsome but empathetic and instantly likeable. People relish his company. As the biographer Victoria Glendinning says, 'When Colin walks into a room you think GOOD!' In his first book, *Mirror to Damascus* (1967), even a Mother Superior opens the doors of her convent and invites him to stay among her nuns.

So how did it all begin? 'The love of words came before the love of travel. I was in love with words from the age of about 8,' says Thubron, 'doubtless influenced by my mother's connection with John Dryden: he was her collateral ancestor.' But, well into his teens, he saw a future for himself as a poet and novelist. Then, when he was 19, his sister – and only sibling – Carol was killed in a skiing accident.

His parents took him on a long holiday in the Middle East 'as a way of escaping sadness'. Somewhere near Damascus, their camper van broke down. Mr and Mrs Thubron stayed put, but Colin took himself into the city to explore. 'I became fascinated with urban culture – with the history and the architecture. I would walk about peering through doors that had been left open, looking through to marble- and basalt-paved courtyards with lemon trees and fountains. It was a world sufficiently attached to what I knew – it had a

relevance to European history – but also exotic and strange.' The idea of travel writing took root. Was it an escape? 'Absolutely not. For me, staying at home is much more to do with escape.'

Thubron's wife, Margreta, is unfazed by his lengthy absences from home, and by the fact that, when he sets off for the Amur river, he won't be taking a mobile phone. And when he returns, she will give him space as he works 'with a slightly crazy stamina', turning his notes into a book. Margreta is a Shakespearean scholar, 'and she too works long hours and very intensely. She's not in the background wanting to go to a party, or a play. So we just turn down invitations and work solidly from 9 to 9.'

Though few could match Thubron for courage, perseverance, intelligence and sensitivity, it's hard not to think that his has been a charmed existence. But much has changed since he set out as a travel writer half a century ago. Damascus, the city that first fired his imagination, and where he found the people 'intoxicatingly hospitable to this naïve and enthusiastic young man', has been transformed by war, and by the crises that have afflicted the Middle East during the last fifty years – 'the conflicts with Israel, the eclipse of war-torn Beirut, the impact of the Arab Spring'. And every part of the world has come under the homogenizing influence of Westernization. How does he respond when, as sometimes happens, a young person confesses that he too longs to be a travel writer?

'One would have to say it would be difficult,' Thubron deliberates,

especially if he was serious, by which I mean if he was a writer as well as a traveller (a traveller who just does a tough voyage has never much interested me). But at the same time the fact that the world appears to be getting smaller and more accessible is to some extent an illusion. The world is known, but only superficially. The Westernization of the world is a superficial thing. Cultures are tremendously resilient, and the future of travel writing is in stripping away the apparent accessibility and Westernization and finding what's distinctive underneath. It's all still there, sitting there, waiting.

MAGGIE FERGUSSON is Literary Editor of *The Tablet*, and Literary Director of the Royal Society of Literature.

# An Epic Achievement

CHRISTOPHER RUSH

I first learned about Adam and Eve, and about Satan and the serpent, when I was scarcely old enough to walk, let alone talk. I know this because both my biblical and literary education were undertaken by Epp, the great-great-aunt who was also our landlady in our Scottish fishing-village home in the 1940s, and with whom I was left when my parents were working. Epp died when I was 3, and I was shown her in her coffin.

If Epp mentioned Milton I don't remember it. Our first lesson on Eden was scriptural rather than literary – straight from Genesis, an account embellished by Epp with assurances that this very same Satan who had tempted Eve and precipitated the Fall of Man, was not averse to scooping up smaller fry such as myself. But Milton soon got his foot in the door. Epp had a sideboard whose doors and drawers I was not allowed to open. After she died my parents were given the task of gutting the house of its unwanted contents, even down to the chamber pot beneath her bed. And I got into the sideboard.

Among the few books in it was an edition of *Paradise Lost* illustrated by Gustave Doré. It was not a book as such but had been collected unbound by Epp in twelve large-size fortnightly parts (a magazine for each book of the poem) with all the illustrations intact,

John Milton, *Paradise Lost* (1667)
Oxford University Press · Pb · 368pp · £8.99 · ISBN 9780199535743
John Carey's abridgement, *The Essential Paradise Lost* (2017), is available as a
Faber hardback: 256pp · £16.99 · ISBN 9780571328550.

and with tipped-in coloured Edwardian adverts for Lux and Lifebuoy and other household products.

A picture is the literature of the illiterate, and I was transfixed by those cosmic scenes. But what made the profoundest impression on me were the pictures of Adam and Eve, so strangely vulnerable in their nakedness. There was something about the naked pair that seemed to say something about the human situation, something I couldn't articulate, couldn't even conceive, but even in my infancy, glimpsing Milton through Doré's magic windows, I knew that I was staring at something rich and strange.

*Paradise Lost* was first published 350 years ago in 1667, and was still being hailed and even enjoyed as an epic achievement (literally) into the early twentieth century. Now it's almost unread, except by the chosen academic few. Why? The real problem, says John Carey in his recent abridgement, is not its world picture but quite simply its length. Milton had just turned 20 when he first announced his epic intention, to compose a poem that would encompass all space and time: an ambitious aim, and, as it took another thirty years to accomplish-

Gustave Doré

lish, the resulting work was never going to be short. Even so, eleven and a half thousand lines of blank verse is quite a challenge. But it's not only worth the read – not to experience it has been compared to cutting Shakespeare or Beethoven out of your life. Imagine.

For those who don't know: the story of the poem is that of the creation of the universe, the rebellion against God by Satan and his fellow fallen angels, followed by the Genesis account of the Fall of Man after Adam and Eve are tempted by the serpent (Satan in disguise) to disobey God by eating the fruit of the forbidden tree, popularly an apple, and are evicted from the Garden of Eden and condemned to a life of hard labour (Adam) and childbearing (Eve). The poem acknowledges therefore the triumph of evil and the loss of innocence, the curse of work followed by the curse of death, all of us now doomed to return to the dust from whence we came.

Naturally Satan will be punished and humanity redeemed – if it chooses to be – but the ending of the poem stays intractably true to the title: Adam and Eve are unparadised; they are now refugees, and are turned out naked into the world. And yet – Milton may not have been the first to say it but he said it more movingly than anyone else – they have each other. And it was that picture of the disconsolate couple, evicted from their home, scantily clad and facing an unknown future, but still together, which all those years ago touched something in my infant mind:

> The world was all before them, where to choose
> Their place of rest, and providence their guide;
> They hand in hand with wandering steps and slow,
> Through Eden took their solitary way.

My heart went out to them; I didn't need to read the verse to feel it; I didn't know it at the time but I was feeling sorry for *myself*. Milton's poem is about all of us, and what has become of us, or what will become of us. Almost certainly.

Which is what makes it essential reading. It doesn't matter if you are not a fundamentalist, not a creationist, if you don't care for Hebrew mythology, or if you don't even believe in God. Do you have to believe in Zeus to enjoy the *Odyssey*? Odysseus himself is no saint and in *Paradise Lost* there is a similar ambivalence about good and evil which may stem from the astonishing process of its poetic creation.

Because the curious thing about *Paradise Lost* is that Milton didn't write it: Urania did. And who was Urania? She was his heavenly muse, who dictated the poem to him in sections while he was asleep, and when he awoke he in turn dictated the night-shift's production to whomsoever happened to be on hand to take it down. A likely story? There were no witnesses to what went on in Milton's unconscious mind, but no lack of them to testify to the ready-made blocks of blank verse that arrived each morning through the ethereal post, or to the incontestable fact that the poet couldn't come up with a single line of poetry for this particular poem when he was awake.

If it still sounds far-fetched, it's not the only instance among poets of unconscious creativity. 'Kubla Khan' is an iconic example, and William Blake's house in London famously teemed with divine visitants: spirits who dictated poems, and angels who obligingly sat for their portraits. Milton's Urania sounds like small fry by comparison, a bit like the tooth fairy – except of course for the sheer size of the sixpence.

Whether you argue, like John Carey, that the two different Miltons you encounter in *Paradise Lost* could be the result of this conscious-unconscious process of composition, or whether it stems from a split personality, or simply from opposing emotions, there is no doubt that Milton appears unconsciously opposed to the very God he consciously extols, with his secret self on the side of the rebel angels, and in particular Satan.

And the paradox deepens. At one point in the poem, while he hails the light which God brought into the darkness, Milton gives way to a passage of self-pity, regretting, even lamenting, his early blindness, and the darkness to which he feels he has been unjustly condemned. The fellowship felt with other blind poets is small consolation. Nature has its cycle, but the blind man knows no rotation, no rhythm, no soothing sequence:

> Thus with the year
> Seasons return, but not to me returns
> Day, or the sweet approach of even or morn,

> Or sight of vernal bloom, or summer's rose,
> Or flocks, or herds, or human face divine;
> But cloud instead, and ever-during dark
> Surrounds me, from the cheerful ways of men
> Cut off.

And the blindness was not all of it. During the years he was planning and writing, or 'receiving', the great work, his life had been far from easy. He'd been unhappily married; had lost two children in infancy, including his only son; lost also his beloved second wife ('my late espoused saint') and their infant daughter within weeks of one another; Cromwell died in September of that year; and following the Restoration, when the anti-monarchists were being hunted down and disembowelled, Milton was arrested and imprisoned, escaping the threat of execution thanks to friends, but seeing his books instead face the common hangman, by whom they were publicly burned, while he himself was ridiculed and vilified: the republic was at an end, paradise had indeed been lost. It's hard not to detect a note of unconscious hostility to God when he contemplates these bitter injustices; and while on the surface he accepts and extols, underneath there is this rankling, which is yet another of the poem's dichotomies: it is no mere Puritan tract or statement of smug dogma.

Nor are Adam and Eve the cardboard cut-outs you might suppose; on the contrary they are interestingly differentiated. Eve is beguiled by the wily words of the serpent, appealing to her vanity, and she sins almost absentmindedly. Adam sins deliberately, declaring his devotion to her, for better or worse, to be stronger than his obedience to God, and so if she is to be cast out, if she is to die, so will he: he can't live without her. Epp never told me this, and she never told me because it's not in Genesis. Milton made it up, which meant it was not the word of God. But he made it up because he was a poet, and in doing so he penned one of the most moving passages in literature, of which I can only quote part here:

O fairest of creation, last and best
Of all God's works . . . with thee
Certain my resolution is to die;
How can I live without thee, how forgo
Thy sweet converse and love so dearly joined,
To live again in these wild woods forlorn?
Should God create another Eve, and I
Another rib afford, yet loss of thee
Would never from my heart; no no, I feel
The link of nature draw me: flesh of flesh,
Bone of my bone thou art, and from thy state
Mine never shall be parted, bliss or woe.

Twenty lines in this vein, followed by another forty, and ending with the starkly moving: 'to lose thee were to lose myself'. Its only equivalent in literature is Catherine Earnshaw's 'I *am* Heathcliff.' Greatest sinner, then? Or greatest lover? Another imponderable paradox. There is more than one sacrifice at the heart of this poem: it's an entirely new kind of epic.

And one other thing above all else: what happens in *Paradise Lost* needn't have happened – it could have been avoided. At an astonishing moment in the poem Satan is depicted gazing at Eve and finding himself stunned by her beauty and innocence. So there was that moment when he could have pulled back. As could Eve. As could Adam. Here is Milton showing us more clearly than any other writer that life is ultimately about making choices. Satan is free to choose – as are we all – and he chooses the evil option, the one that suits his own ignoble ends. It's a nakedly revealing moment and, with Adam and Eve's, the most momentous in literature.

That freedom is vital and their ignorance is bliss so long as they obey God's one explicit order; or disobey and face the music: the still sad music of humanity. I once had a chemistry teacher whom we nicknamed, ironically enough, the Lord God, and who used to say to us: 'Lick this and you'll be pushing up daisies.' God doesn't put it in quite those words but the message is the same: on pain of death. It doesn't do to be too doctrinaire about the meaning of the message here, but there's a Faustian one for sure: knowledge is power; power corrupts; absolute power corrupts absolutely; and if you want to make the Faustian pact with life and listen to the insidious Mephistophelian whispering in your ear, *And I said, ye shall be as gods*, then you'll end up in trouble – one way or another pushing up daisies.

You don't have to be a Puritan to appreciate this poem; you don't have to be a republican, or a monarchist; you don't even have to be religious; you don't have to be anything. The poem is deeply embedded in theology, but its emotional message is not dependent on it. And what is that message? Choice, yes, most certainly. But there is something else. All human beings know or have known what it is to be Adam and Eve; all of us have had our Edens, our lost paradises, whether they be love, prosperity, innocence, idealism, power, health and strength, childhood, youth, dreams. All unhappiness springs from loss. Sometimes it's loss of what you want and can never have: mostly it's the more haunting form of loss – loss of what you once had and can never have again. This has nothing to do with gods or devils or religious beliefs, it's about human life. *Paradise Lost* is about ourselves.

CHRISTOPHER RUSH has been writing for thirty-five years. His books include the memoirs *To Travel Hopefully* and *Hellfire and Herring*, and *Will*, a novel about Shakespeare. His latest novel, *Penelope's Web*, was published in 2015.

# Pony-mad

JULIE WELCH

 Did your mother, like mine, throw them out in the end? They stayed on the bookshelves in my old bedroom long after I'd left home, waiting for the next generation of girls to join our family, but my sister and I produced boy after boy. When, after my mother died, I cleared out her house, I looked for my Jill books, but they were all gone.

Ruby Ferguson wrote nine 'Jill' books, of which *Jill's Gymkhana* is the first. Originally published in 1949 by Hodder & Stoughton, it was beautifully illustrated by 'Caney', and priced at 7s 6d. A review by Frances Vivien in the *Observer* of 9 May that year declared it 'a perfect pony story for girls'.

Why did I need the books? Well, I was putting together a talk for a girls' school on how I became a sportswriter. This meant retracing a route back through teenage crushes on footballers, to watching the horse-racing on Saturday afternoons with my father, to my pre-pubescent pony mania when Jill was my first role model.

It began on the summer morning in 1955 when our family moved house. While the pantechnicon was being unloaded, a diminutive girl with freckles and a corolla of tawny curls strolled along from the

---

Ruby Ferguson, *Jill's Gymkhana* (1949), *A Stable for Jill* (1951), *Jill Has Two Ponies* (1952), *Jill Enjoys Her Ponies* (1954), *Rosettes for Jill* (1957), *Jill and the Perfect Pony* (1959), *Pony Jobs for Jill* (1960) and *Jill's Pony Trek* (1962), are all out of print but we can obtain second-hand copies. *Jill's Riding Club* (1956) is available from Fidra Books · Pb · 210pp · £7.99 · ISBN 9781906123291.

house next door. I recognized her; we were at the same school and her name was Jo, but we had never spoken because she was in the form above me. Nor did we speak now. She bypassed me and went directly to my mother: 'Would Julia like to play?'

My mother explained that I had chickenpox and in consequence was confined with my spots and germs in the back of the family saloon. 'Oh, that's all right,' said the world's most self-assured 8-year-old. 'I've had it. You can't get it twice, you know.' She tapped on the car window to get my attention: 'Do you ride?'

'Oh gosh, yes,' I said excitedly, while mentally crossing my fingers since my sole experience had been a humiliating episode in which a pony called Snowball had bolted with me when I was 4. I'd grabbed a strand of barbed wire as a handbrake: six and a half decades on, the scar is still visible, a faint, pale forward slash on my middle finger.

But off I went with Jo to the Buckhurst Hill Riding School: two lessons a week, eight shillings a go. Jo must have seen through my fib because I fell off a lot, but she had obviously decided to mentor me. 'There's a book you might enjoy called *Jill's Gymkhana*,' she said. 'It's about learning to ride.'

It was about more than that. I grew up during the great post-Second World War era of pony books and eventually my shelves included almost every title in print, from Monica Edwards's Romney Marsh books and the American series by Mary O'Hara that began with *My Friend Flicka*, to the entire output of the Pullein-Thompson sisters, Christine, Diana and Josephine (a horsey version of the Brontës though a good deal more cheerful). But the 'Jills' were the first, best-loved and most frequently reread. They were witty and irreverent, did not talk down, and introduced me to one of the greatest joys of novel-reading, that sudden moment of self-recognition – 'Yes, that's exactly how I feel.'

Ruby Ferguson was already an established author when she wrote them but, in the same way that Richmal Crompton wrote bags of novels for adults but had to settle for immortality via *Just William*, her earlier output of mysteries and romantic fiction is now pretty well forgotten. Born Ruby Ashby in Hebden Bridge, Yorkshire, in 1899, the daughter of a Wesleyan Methodist minister, she was educated at the Girls' Grammar School, Bradford, and left St Hilda's, Oxford, in 1922 with a degree in English Literature. What a lot of dreary jobs brainy women had to settle for back then. For a while she was a secretary; then she did some teaching and worked in a political organization. She loathed both, but at least they allowed her to do some writing. Her first break came when *Manchester City News* took a series of her short detective stories, after which she edited the Woman's Page of *British Weekly*. At one point she was a staffer on the *Manchester Guardian* and moonlighted as a reader for Hodder & Stoughton. They were to be her chief publishers.

Part of the generation that lost all its men, she did not marry until her mid-thirties. Her husband, Samuel Ferguson, was a comfortably-off widower with two grown-up sons, Bobbie and Alan, with whom she got on well. She was 50 when she embarked on the Jill books, which she wrote for Bobbie's four daughters, the oldest three of whom appear as the rambunctious April, May and June Cholly-Sawcutt. Jill teaches them to ride in *Jill Has Two Ponies*, number three in the running order.

It's possible to go into such detail because of some fine detective work by Alison Haywards, whose article on the author appeared in the Newsletter of the Children's Books History Society for April 2005. The text is accessible thanks to Jane Badger, author of *Heroines on Horseback: The Pony Book in Children's Fiction*, who has a glorious website dedicated to the genre (just Google Jane Badger Books). By the time I found it, I had already shopped on line for *Jill's Gymkhana*. Having boggled at the cost of early-edition hardbacks, I settled for a 1985 Knight paperback. It had a not very interesting photo cover, but it would have to do.

As soon as I looked inside I had a shock. I knew that when Knight, the paperback division of Hodder & Stoughton, had taken on the Jill books they had changed the name of her pony Black Boy to Danny Boy. Subsequently they relented, and I was delighted to find that in my version he was Black Boy once again. What I wasn't prepared for was a second change that had not been amended. Black Boy was . . . a piebald? Surely not. I was outraged, gripped by a kind of near-Aspergic literalism. How could you call a piebald pony Black Boy? Had I remembered it wrong? I couldn't have. Black Boy was, with Jill, the book's main character – 'sturdy but graceful, about fourteen hands, with a nice action and very intelligent face'. He had velvety lips and loved carrots, apples and jumping. And he was black.

Thank goodness for Jane Badger's website. Here I found thumbnails of the original covers, and here it was, the Caney illustration I remembered of Jill in her brown hacking jacket and fawn jodhpurs astride Black Boy, a red rosette fluttering on his bridle, his coat as black as an old LP. The original Black Boy was not a piebald. The publisher must have changed his colour when they renamed him Danny Boy. My memory hadn't been at fault. What a relief.

So, *Jill's Gymkhana.* Here's the plot. Eleven-year-old Jill Crewe has come to live in reduced circumstances with her mother in a village called Chatton. A briskly dealt with tragedy has whisked Mr Crewe out of the picture, and gallant, principled Mummy holds the tent up by writing dreadfully twee books for children. Jill cannot ride so, in horse-mad Chatton, she is ostracized, but she befriends a pony, the aforementioned Black Boy. His owner, Farmer Clay, offers to sell him for £25, which is well beyond Jill's means, but life takes a turn for the better when Mummy sells the serial rights to *The Little House of Smiles.*

Mummy shares some of the bounty with Jill ('Thirty pounds! Oh crumbs!') and she buys Black Boy. The story – told, like the other books, in the first person – follows Jill and her best friend Ann Derry through a series of adventures as she learns, with the help of Martin Lowe, a wheelchair-bound former RAF pilot, to ride Black Boy and care for him ('everyone knows that the best quality soap-flakes are the nicest thing for washing a horse's tail'). She has to earn the money for his keep, resulting at one point in an amusingly doomed Bring and Buy sale, and she turns an outhouse into a stable ('all sensible people know that really messy manual labour is one of the jolliest things in the world, when you are dressed for it and it doesn't matter how filthy you get').

Boys, of course, she treats as equals, rather than Gods Come Down: 'Even if you are sixteen you're not all that marvellous,' she tells Martin's supercilious nephew, Pierce. The male characters though, while benevolent, don't come to life in the way the females do. Ann Derry's mother is crisply described as 'living in a perpetual state of thinking there's going to be a disaster', and the slightly fearsome Mrs Darcy, owner of one of Chatton's riding schools, 'was the sort of person who always seemed to have an exclamation mark after everything she said; that is why I have put one'.

Jill's enemy is the snooty Susan Pyke, who has rich parents and a string of effortlessly superior ponies, and who leads the laughter at Jill's initial attempts to ride. I had a Susan Pyke in my life. She mocked the elastic-waisted trews and school lace-ups in which I turned up for early riding lessons, my mother having deferred kitting me out properly until I'd proved this was more than a phase. Susan, of course, wears 'a perfect black jacket and cream cord breeches, and black boots, and a white shirt and yellow tie, and a new hat and cream string gloves'.

To show off her trophies and her latest pony, Susan invites Jill and Ann to tea. *Chez* Pyke, they meet Susan's mother, 'who was majestic and had a deep voice'.

> 'When I was a child,' said Mrs Pyke, 'I was the youngest rider to hounds in the county. I remember the MFH once lifted me on to my pony himself, and there I sat in my little habit with my long fair curls hanging down to my waist.'

Soon Susan is satisfyingly shown up at the Lentham Park Children's

Gymkhana, where she whips her pony about the head and is ordered from the ring by the judge. Jill triumphs ultimately with a clear round and first prize in the under-16s jumping at Chatton Show:

> I was frightfully happy, of course, but I didn't feel the least bit cocky or conceited, because I knew that I'd had a lot of luck . . . And I have written this book to show what a quite ordinary person can do with a quite ordinary pony, if he or she really cares about riding.

I can't be the only Jill enthusiast who wishes she still had the original, as well as its sequels. I made do with the thumbnails of the covers on Jane Badger's website. They were my equivalent of Proust's madeleine. I relived my hauntings of the bookshop in Loughton High Street in the hope of a Jill book I had not yet read; my dreams of competing, just like Jill, at the Horse of the Year Show at the Harringay Arena; the joys of reading in the bath with *Jill Enjoys Her Ponies*, the publication of which coincided with the arrival in our household of the bath tray, a metal rack that had enough room for a book to be propped alongside soap and flannel. I remembered that the name of one character, Mercy Dulbottle (a bit of a drip), had made me giggle so much I *crawled on the floor*. I absolutely did. In *Jill Has Two Ponies* (the title self-explanatory), the name of Jill's new pony is Rapide. I can still hear my big sister cackling with laughter when I pronounced Rapide 'Rap-eyed' (because, as Jill observes, 'the most shattering thing in the world is being laughed at').

But what would a 9-year-old of today make of them? Would they seem dated, even off-putting, with their tacit approval of hunting? The language is of their (and my) time, when people were 'jolly decent', when if something nice happened you were 'frightfully bucked', and when people exclaimed, 'Gosh!' and 'Oh, rather!' The tea bell with which Mummy summons Jill and Ann must be as obsolete as other artefacts of a mid-twentieth-century childhood, like combinations and cod-liver oil, and surely no one has eaten sardine sandwiches since 1979. But then again, Enid Blyton's school stories, where everyone goshes and gollies like mad, are still in print, relished by new generations of little girls. And anyway, ponies don't date.

So then I did some more digging around on the Internet and discovered that reprints had been available recently from Fidra Books, although, disappointingly, only *Jill's Riding Club* was on offer when I looked. But one way and another they have stayed in print longer than any other series of pony books. I think it's because Jill is such an engaging character. Self-reliant, enterprising, honourable and full of joie de vivre, she is a wonderful example of how to be a girl. A few weeks after its arrival, I received an email from the online bookseller: 'Julia, did *Jill's Gymkhana* by Ruby Ferguson live up to your expectations?' Oh gosh, yes.

JULIE WELCH was Fleet Street's first female football reporter. Her memoir of boarding-school life in the 1960s, *Too Marvellous for Words*, is published by Simon & Schuster.

# Hands across the Tea-shop Table

SUE GEE

Sometimes in the long summer's evenings, which are so marked
a part of our youth, Harriet and Vesey played hide-and-seek
with the younger children, running across the tufted meadows,
their shoes yellow with the pollen of buttercups. They could not
run fast across those uneven fields; nor did they wish to, since
to find the hiding children was to lose their time together, to
run faster was to run away from one another. The jog-trot was
a game devised from shyness and uncertainty. Neither dared to
assume that the other wished to pause and inexperience barred
them both from testing this.

I first read *A Game of Hide and Seek* in my teens, at about the same
age as Harriet and Vesey, running through the buttercup field in
those opening lines, and I loved it so much that it hurt. For years I
could hardly look at the dust jacket on the Book Club edition of 1951,
given to my mother by her favourite niece, without an ache of the
sadness and longing which Elizabeth Taylor so powerfully evokes in
the story of two people who have always loved one another, but who
will never be together.

I read it again in my thirties and still fell under its spell. One
might despise Vesey, as other characters do, for his strangeness – his
very name; his unappetizing white skin, gnat-bitten on those summer

Elizabeth Taylor, *A Game of Hide and Seek* (1951)
Virago · Pb · 320pp · £8.99 · ISBN 9781844086191
Nicola Beauman, *The Other Elizabeth Taylor* (2009)
Persephone · Pb · 448pp · £15 · ISBN 9781906462109

evenings; his casual rudeness and cruelties, both to the family with whom he stays in school holidays and to Harriet, who loves him so – and yet, like Harriet, I found him mesmerizing.

With the publication in 2009 of Nicola Beauman's excellent biography, *The Other Elizabeth Taylor*, I read the novel again, and this time was disenchanted. It felt stiff, contrived, full of set pieces. But this year, in Philip Hensher's Penguin collection of British short stories, I came upon Taylor's gloriously sharp and funny 'In and Out the Houses', in which she portrays the vicissitudes of village life through the activities of a clever little girl. Once more I reread *A Game of Hide and Seek* – set in a Buckinghamshire village and market town. I remembered its visceral importance in my younger days, and knew I must write about it.

The novel is set in the 1920s and 1940s. Both world wars are elided, the one before it opens, the other between one chapter and the next, but in the background is the fierce struggle of the suffragettes, when Lilian, Harriet's mother, had been sent to prison. A clever, principled woman, widowed young, she despairs of her daughter, who has left school without an exam or an ambition, and sends her to help look after the two children of Caroline Macmillan, one-time fellow suffragette, still dearest friend. It is in this worthy, book-lined, vegetarian household that Harriet falls for Vesey, nephew of Caroline's husband.

Vesey is waiting to go up to Oxford. His father has long been absent; his mother, a London beautician, has long neglected him. Like Harriet he is directionless, unmoored; unlike her, he is educated and clever, confessing to her that his real ambition is to be a writer. All her focus during this summer is on him, but for much of the time she has no idea if her feelings are reciprocated. By turns he is languid, mischievous (encouraging the children to eat meat on an outing), teasing, suddenly perceptive. They walk and talk; the children are always with them. One afternoon they come upon a deserted old house and, in a sunlit, dusty bedroom, exchange a passionate kiss.

Neither can quite believe this has happened. But within two days Caroline, discovering the meat episode, has asked Vesey to leave. Suddenly awkward again, their goodbyes are polite exchanges.

Harriet mourns terribly, hears nothing. She goes to work in a gown shop: a vividly written episode with past-it older women taking a keen interest in their younger colleague – particularly once she begins to go out with Charles Jephcott. He, a solicitor with a broken engagement behind him, has come to live in the village with his mother Julia, a retired actress clinging to past glories. She invites Lilian and Harriet to tea; Charles falls for Harriet's innocence and lost air; when her mother becomes suddenly ill and dies, she knows he will look after her. In a very short time they are married.

When we meet her again, Harriet is transformed. A mature, well-read and accomplished wife and mother, she runs a lovely home, complete with mother's help and cleaning lady; gives dinner parties, sits on committees, attends meetings at her daughter Betsy's school.

This comfortable, ordered life is disturbed when Vesey – who dropped out of Oxford – reappears. He has become not a writer but an actor, living an impoverished life in rep: *Hamlet* has come to Market Swanford. They meet again; Harriet takes Betsy to the play. And now the unspoken love of their youth is unstoppably reignited.

In this story of a provincial married woman who longs for what she cannot have, two great literary influences are immediately apparent. One is *Madame Bovary*, the other *Brief Encounter*. That unforgettable film clearly stands behind all the snatched and secret meetings Harriet and Vesey have in London, where he has his wretched digs: the railway station and freezing trains, the foggy lamp-lit streets, the hands across the tea-shop table. It stands, too, behind the agonized conversations between Harriet and good, solid, wounded Charles.

Elizabeth Taylor saw the film in 1946, but the origins of the love triangle explored in *A Game of Hide and Seek* lie far deeper. She spent much of her life fending off questions about the relationship between her life and her books, and with good reason.

Elizabeth Taylor by Rodrigo Moynihan, early 1950s

A complex, clever, interesting woman, she was, in her early twenties, something of a free spirit, a creative person in embryo. She tutored the bright little son of Dilwyn Knox (see *SF* no. 49) and made herself useful at Pigotts, the nearby studio of Eric Gill. Surprisingly, she then married, as Nicola Beauman eloquently puts it, not the corduroy trousers of a bohemian but the *Daily Telegraph*. In 1936 she became the wife of John Taylor, the respectable, well-off son of a local sweet manufacturer. In that same year she joined the Communist Party.

Set against the domestic intimacies of her fiction, this fact is also startling. But perhaps Pigotts had radicalized her, and, though 'never a joiner', she was clear about her reasons. 'I did not see why economic freedom would not lead to the other more important liberties – of speech and thought and expression,' she wrote after the war, and she threw herself into meetings, selling the *Daily Worker* on the streets of High Wycombe with a young working-class comrade, Ray Russell. Within a year, she had fallen deeply in love. 'I didn't know I had the capacity for loving anyone as I love you,' she wrote to him, and she continued to love him for years, while outwardly living the life of a writer who was also a contented wife and mother.

It was a meeting of minds, as well as a passionate affair, and their long conversations explored questions of artistic practice, as well as politics. She joined the Left Book Club and for a long time felt that her own (so far unpublished) writing should be politically engaged. But in 1943 she wrote to Ray, 'What utter cock it all was. We had only to look around us to see what literature *is*. What it does *not* do is reflect contemporary history. All the great novels shriek this to the housetops . . . Only private life is there, how this and that person lived.' She left the Party in 1948.

And in 1951 *A Game of Hide and Seek* appeared, its focus almost exclusively on the private life, on a woman torn – as she herself must have been – between the claims of duty and passion. 'An un-eventful life, thank God,' she told the world, concealing what was perhaps the greatest event of her life. It found its coded way into this novel, which Elizabeth Bowen hailed as her finest.

> **ELIZABETH**
> # TAYLOR
> *A Game of Hide & Seek*
>
> " Her finest novel "    E. Bowen
> " Exquisite "    Richard Church
> " Exquisite "    E. V. Knox
> " Real poetry "    John Betjeman
> " A masterpiece "    Nancy Spain
> " Genius "    Marghanita Laski
> " Genius "    Vernon Fane
> " Genius "    S. P. B. Mais
>
> Selling everywhere  9/6
>
> *Peter Davies*

Not everyone agreed. Blanche Knopf, her US editor, wanted many minor characters cut out, and the focus to be tighter. And after all my rereadings, I do find it flawed. There are small but abrasive careless-nesses: Betsy, the daughter, has her own long story, but unaccountably she is not in the house during a crucial scene between her parents. It is as if she had never existed. Then, on the rain-swept journey to their first weekend away, Harriet tells Vesey, 'All my relations are near Oxford.' Really? Who they? Until now she has been presented as quite without family once her mother has died.

One or two larger things are unconvincing. So sensitively has Taylor portrayed Harriet as a hesitant, yearning, uneducated adolescent that it's hard to believe that in adult life she becomes so mature in her duties. Would she not shrink from meetings with Betsy's teachers, when her own schooldays had been so hopeless? Would she really be a useful committee person?

And so on. Yet, as a novel of its times, it still has extraordinary power. Taylor's great strength is atmosphere – a hallmark of romantic fiction, and this is undeniably a romantic novel. And if one had to point to one moment in the whole which lifts it above so much else, it is the ending. I shall not reveal it, but only say that the uncertainty all at once stirred by those subtle Chekhovian lines (and Chekhov was another great influence on Elizabeth Taylor) is indeed a masterstroke.

SUE GEE's latest novel, *Trio*, features a group of young musicians in the 1930s, and is undeniably romantic.

# *Marcel*

ANTHONY WELLS

In my earlier pieces on Marcel Proust's *Remembrance of Things Past* (*SF* nos. 56 and 57) I looked at different aspects of the novel as embodied, first, in the character of Charles Swann and then in the family of the Guermantes, the *crème de la crème* of the French aristocracy. It is now time to turn to the central figure in the novel, the narrator himself, the author of this fictional autobiography.

Stretching over seven books and amounting to more than 3,000 pages, Proust's novel opens with the narrator remembering times when, as a boy, he stayed with his parents, his grandmother and their housekeeper, Françoise, in his great-aunt's house in the village of Combray. We are not told at any stage what age this boy is, nor what he is called. We are plunged only into the boy's mind and feelings – when he is told a story by his aunt illustrated by magic-lantern slides projected on to his bedroom curtains, or when he sits in the garden of the house reading the novels of his favourite author, Bergotte, or when he lies awake in a state of panic on the evenings when the presence of a guest at the family supper table might mean that his mother will not come up to give him his goodnight kiss, and he will be unable to sleep.

We gather quite quickly, from what the narrator tells us both about himself and about the attitudes taken to him by his family, that

The first English translation, by C. K. Scott Moncrieff, is available from Vintage in six paperbacks. It is also available in hardback, in a four-volume boxed set, from Everyman at £65 (ISBN 9781857152500). A new translation by several hands is available from Penguin, also in six paperbacks.

he is a sickly child, probably a chronic asthmatic, certainly prone to breathlessness and panic attacks, tearful, clinging, a mummy's boy, cossetted, perhaps, and overprotected. His grandmother, while anxious to encourage his precocious intellectual and artistic interests with gifts of classic novels and postcards of famous paintings, constantly recommends more fresh air and exercise for the boy, while his mother tries to wean him off his dependence on her goodnight kiss, in an attempt to strengthen his will and encourage more independence. The narrator then describes one night in particular, a night when his parents' friend M. Swann comes to supper, and his father, who is impatient with these childish rituals, at first refuses to permit the boy's mother to go upstairs to deliver the goodnight kiss but then unexpectedly changes his mind, agreeing to her not only giving him his kiss but even spending the night with the boy.

This dramatic night of his boyhood is recalled on repeated occasions during the novel, as if it were a key both to his suffering in later years at the hands of the girls and women he falls in love with, and to his failures of willpower in regard to the work he must finally settle down to. In many other ways, too, the opening book, *The Way by Swann's*, is the seed, or bulb, from which the remaining six books and hundreds of pages grow, and within which their entire structure, colour and texture are adumbrated. Like the overture of a great opera, *The Way by Swann's* contains all the themes that will be developed at much greater length, and with greater variety, and subtlety, in the remainder of the work, as well as introducing us to very many of the characters whose lives we will follow. And just as it is possible to listen to an overture – to *The Marriage of Figaro* or *Die Meistersinger* – as a separate piece of music, so *The Way by Swann's* can be read on its own, since it has its own sense of completeness.

So, in one way, it is little wonder that some readers get to the end of *The Way by Swann's* and then stop. Others who persevere beyond the first book break off at some later stage, meaning to return but never finding the time. There are reasons for this, too. The novel is not an easy read. Proust's sentences can be long, very long; his paragraphs can cover pages. (It has been difficult to find suitable quotations for this very reason.) The narrator is much given to reflection, and takes advantage of his captive audience, his readers, to reflect at length. The book demands patience; it has to be taken slowly.

It is also, as an acquaintance recently said of a different novel, 'very French'. Not only are the names of the characters, the streets, the villages and towns French, the historical and literary references are mostly French, and the quotations are from French poems and plays. Racine's tragedy of jealous obsession, *Phèdre*, is one running motif of the novel, as are his later religious plays *Esther* and *Athalie*, but while we have heard of and possibly seen the first, the second and third are barely known even to the most cultivated English readers. There are other things about the novel that can seem off-putting. The narrator himself is in many respects not particularly admirable and can come across as arrogant and with an intellectual superiority complex.

But those who do set the novel aside early are missing out on one of the greatest experiences literature has to offer. Doing so is comparable to visiting one of the great cathedrals and seeing only the façade, without going inside to appreciate the soaring columns, the tracery of the roof and the brilliant stained glass. However trying the narrator may be from time to time, whatever the *longueurs* of certain sections, the novel is as great a work as a cathedral and the narrator is the guide making sense of it all. For, as well as being a social history of France in the period 1870–1920, Proust's novel is the history of a single life of that period (or two lives, if we include Swann) and it is through the narrator's eyes and mind that we experience the times. Through the narrator Proust introduces the element of subjective experience into the story, so that reading the novel through the medium of the narrator's thoughts echoes our own experience of life as we live it.

As the narrator keeps stressing, other people are a mystery, we know them only from the outside, we have to piece their thoughts and characters together from their words and actions. So other people can defy expectations, do surprising things, fall in love with the last people we thought they would, including members of their own sex, and be capable of producing great work – paintings or music that may survive for centuries, for instance – despite the nullity of their conversation and the obscurity of their lives. People also change, their characters are not static: a chance meeting or event can awaken unsuspected sides to them, and unearth motives completely hidden up to that point.

These changes take place within the framework of biology, however. The narrator is a student of botany and zoology, he studies his fellow human beings – and himself – like a scientist, his ambition is to discover the laws, or some of them, which underlie human behaviour. The laws of some aspects of psychology, he tells us, are as 'precise as those of hydrostatics'. As he grows older, he observes how more elements of his parents' characters emerge in his own actions.

This fascination with heredity is one of the major reasons he patronizes the salons and spends so much time with the old aristocracy. In the Guermantes and their class he sees both the preservation of characteristics over large spans of time – remarking for example that the Baron de Charlus has attitudes and uses expressions which would not have been out of place at the court of Louis XIV – and the living embodiment of French history. The continuance of the Guermantes family over centuries he sees as a triumph of human survival over the great destroyer, Time. He sees the same triumph of continuity in the family's housekeeper, Françoise, who not only preserves patterns of speech and behaviour present in the French peasantry since time immemorial but whose features echo those portrayed in the sculptures which decorate ancient French churches.

The bourgeois narrator, or Marcel as he is referred to on a couple of occasions, has the pedigree of neither of these classes; he has his intelligence and, he hopes, literary talent. He employs his intelligence without rest in the attempt to understand what other people, and most painfully the objects of his desire, are about and to understand himself. How could he have missed or ignored the signs that his beloved grandmother was so ill? Why is it that he only grieves properly for her some time after her death, when the memory of her is suddenly triggered 'in a complete and involuntary recollection' when, back in the same bedroom of the seaside hotel in Normandy where she had stayed with him years before, he bends down to untie his boots? What is going on in this mind which, as he says at one point, is the only reality?

The understanding of the intelligence can only go so far: the most significant moments in a person's life, the only truly real moments, occur spontaneously, triggered in the memory by an accidental, unforeseen act or gesture through which what had seemed a lost moment of past life is restored. Tasting the famous madeleine crumbled in a spoonful of tea is one such trigger; stepping on an uneven paving stone is another; a spoon striking a plate with exactly the same note as the little bell which sounded when M. Swann came through the garden gate at the house of the narrator's great-aunt in Combray is yet another. Time as we experience it – personal time, not chronological time – is a continuous flow and we are unable to grasp the significance of any of its fleeting moments as they pass.

Only occasionally, when on the receiving end of vivid impressions, like those transmitted by the foaming pink and white blossom of a line of apple trees, or the haunting, fugitive melody of a piece of music, may we be close to grasping the meaning that appears to lie hidden behind them. It is these impressions that the ('Impressionist') painter Elstir perfects his technique to capture, stripping himself, the narrator tells us, of every intellectual notion in order to register the visual impressions more truthfully. The intellect has no direct access to reality: that privilege is reserved for other human powers. Foremost among these is memory, triggered accidentally but overwhelming in its reality, when moments, places and people of the past who appeared to be lost forever return in the rememberer's mind or soul.

Having tried as much as possible not to give away anything of the plot, I will avoid quoting here any of the superb passages in which Proust uses all his wonderful stylistic and literary skill to convey our sense of the fleetingness of time, our regret at its passing, our fear that everything will be lost to oblivion, that nothing, neither we, nor our loved ones, nor our works will survive. A few sentences will have to suffice. The narrator is walking in the Bois de Boulogne in November, thinking back to the time when he used to walk there with Mme Swann.

> The reality I had known no longer existed. That Mme Swann did not arrive exactly the same at the same moment was enough to make the avenue different. The places we have known do not belong solely to the world of space in which we situate them for our greater convenience. They were only a thin slice among contiguous impressions that formed our life at that time; the memory of a certain image is only regret for a certain moment; and houses, roads, avenues are as fleeting, alas, as the years.

These words are from the final paragraph of *The Way by Swann's*, the first book of the novel. It would be such a mistake to make them the last words you ever read of *Remembrance of Things Past*.

ANTHONY WELLS has spent the best part of a lifetime avoiding putting pen to paper, prevaricating with a number of occupations including monitoring East German radio for the BBC, librarianship and running a family business. He hopes it's going to be a case of better late than never.

# Streams of Consciousness

RICHARD PLATT

A soft summer rain cloaked the Concord River with an iridescent mist in the pre-dawn hours of Saturday, 31 August 1839, as two young men, brothers, eased a small boat of their own construction into the water. She was painted blue and green to reflect the element in which she would live, and christened the *Musketaquid* after the name given to this river of many meadows by the indigenous peoples. They boarded her with happy anticipation as she slipped from the muddy ooze of the bank.

Each man was slightly built and just below medium height. The elder of the two, John Thoreau, 24, was a genial, easy-going, eminently likeable man with a talent for friendship; clever, but rather less bookish than his classically educated younger brother, who had recently come down from Harvard. The younger brother, Henry, was of sterner countenance, his demeanour inspired by the Roman stoicism he so admired, though his passions ran deep. Henry was 22 and more respected than liked, though he had a way with children. He had a reputation for extracting absolute obedience from the most recalcitrant boys in his days as a teacher, though he never resorted to the cane, and he had lost a well-paid teaching position for voicing his objections to its use.

Life had been kind to the Thoreau brothers. They were fit, healthy, enjoyed nothing so much as their time together in the open air, and having successfully taken over the Concord Academy, the local pri-

Henry Thoreau, *A Week on the Concord and Merrimack Rivers* (1849)
Penguin · Pb · 368pp · £7.99 · ISBN 9780140434422

vate school where they themselves had been educated, they had cause for optimism. They were finding their place in the world. It was a time to breathe deeply and venture forth with confidence. These would be among the happiest days of Henry Thoreau's all-too-brief life, and would inspire *A Week on the Concord and Merrimack Rivers* (1849).

This is a young man's book, brimful of life, self-confidence, faith and doubt, with just that whiff of paganism Thoreau so enjoyed holding under the noses of his neighbours. We accompany him as he hews wood for his campfire, the chips flying through the summer sun and dancing in pinwheels as they touch the ground. He quotes bits of history and folklore from his voluminous reading as place names along the river ignite memories of frontier heroism, Celtic myth and even minor Greek poets (which he translates himself); he drops a line in the river to catch his dinner and fries it up over a campfire at sunset. Living when a 'natural philosopher' needed little more than eyes to see, ears to hear, a sense of smell, time and patience, Thoreau would make genuine contributions to the study of natural history, yet he saw every creature that soars, swims or saunters, every landscape, with the eyes of a poet.

> The harebell and the *Rhexia Virginica* . . . growing in patches of lively pink flowers on the edge of the meadows, had almost too gay an appearance for the rest of the landscape, like a pink ribbon on the bonnet of a Puritan woman. Asters and goldenrods were the livery which nature wore at present. The latter alone expressed all the ripeness of the season, and shed their mellow lustre over the fields, as if now declining summer's sun had bequeathed its hues to them. It is the floral solstice a little after mid-summer, when the particles of golden light, the sundust, have, as it were, fallen like seeds on the earth, and produced these blossoms.

It is a quietly uneventful journey: there are no life-threatening rapids, no tales of derring-do, no predators stalking our heroes in the dead of night. It is Thoreau's inner journey that takes centre stage, his thoughts moving freely through the vast ocean of Western civilization. There are flowing cataracts of philosophy, poetry (his own and others'), reflections on primitive versus modern man, the nature of God, and the stuff that the best books are made of. There are leisurely interludes down quiet tributaries, with digressions on solitude, conscience and man's place in the hierarchy of the natural world. It is no surprise that Nathaniel Hawthorne, an astute observer who was not easily impressed, wrote of Henry Thoreau: 'Nature, in return for his love, seems to adopt him as her special child, and shows him secrets which few others are allowed to witness . . . I find him a healthy and wholesome man to know.' And so he is.

One is struck by the extraordinary self-sufficiency of the Thoreaus, of the ease and comfort with which they navigate water and woods. The brothers built their river-worthy craft, fifteen feet long, three feet across at the widest point, with two sets of oars and two retractable masts, in seven days (and recall: without power tools). For their trip, which was to take them many miles through a sparsely populated country marked by settlers' graves and the campfire stones of the natives who had murdered those settlers only a generation before, they took buffalo skins to sleep in, a canvas tent, salt, sugar, corn meal, a bit of oil, fishing line, cocoa and a few melons and potatoes. Thoreau's voice is bright, hopeful and seemingly spontaneous, the narrative rendered quietly heroic when we realize that when he wrote this paean to life, years later, he was fighting his way out of a crippling depression.

Soon after their return to Concord, the Thoreaus discovered that they were falling in love with the same woman, Ellen Sewell, whom they had met just the month before. Henry loved no one as he loved John. As he was later to write, 'The only remedy for love is to love more,' and, ever true to his ideals, he gave John his blessing and removed himself from Ellen's society. Ellen's father, convinced that neither of the Thoreau brothers could provide for themselves, much less a wife and family, forbade his daughter from seeing either of them. No woman would ever turn Henry's head again. The journal he had begun two years earlier would eventually fill fourteen volumes, but he would never write Ellen's name or speak of her again.

Soon after the departure of Ellen from their lives, John Thoreau's health began to fail, and his inability to perform his duties as a schoolmaster forced the brothers to close their school. During his convalescence, he cut himself with a rusty razor. He contracted lockjaw and died an agonizing death in Henry's arms two weeks later. His death was so traumatic for Henry that he developed psychosomatic symptoms, and friends feared for his own life. The symptoms eventually abated, but Henry sank into a black depression. For the first time the stoicism which he so valued failed him.

In his distress he turned to his friend Ralph Waldo Emerson, who was the most respected man of letters in America and was fond of young Henry Thoreau. Thoreau had often worked as a handyman for him and as a tutor to his children. Emerson had recently purchased land on the shore of Walden Pond, just one mile from the centre of Concord, and he needed someone to clear it. Thoreau seemed the natural choice for the job. Emerson had also considered building a small cabin on the land in which to write. Thoreau, an accomplished carpenter who had helped build his family's house with his father, asked if he might build a cabin for Emerson with the felled timber. Emerson consented.

Thoreau borrowed an axe and fled to the woods. He was not, as he would have us believe in *Walden*, a cocksure (and rather priggish) young philosopher-king on a quest to search the depths of his soul and solve the Mysteries of Existence and the Meaning of Life. He was coming apart: a young man on the run, from death, disappointment, failure and his own grief. The next two years would be among the most productive of his life, and the first fruit of his literary labours was *A Week on the Concord and Merrimack Rivers*.

Friends had learned never to speak of John in Henry's presence, and nowhere are we told that John was his companion on his river idyll, save for the poignant reference which begins the selection of verse and epigraph that serve as prologue:

> Where'er thou sail'st who sailed with me,
> Though now thou climbest loftier mounts,
> And fairer rivers dost ascend,
> Be thou my Muse, my Brother _____.

Throughout he writes of 'one' and 'the other', but never of 'my brother'. His stoicism, or denial, is in the ascendant. There is no self-pity, no sense of a groping for sanity. Yet for a man who endeavoured to spend his life at a walking pace to such a degree that it was to become a virtual creed, his thoughts race forth, a cleansing, shimmering cataract of effervescence, of exuberant exaltation and wonder. Late in the journey, he reflects on the ideal Friend.

> As surely as the sunset in my latest November shall translate me to the ethereal world, and remind me of the ruddy morning of youth; as surely as the last strain of music which falls on my decaying ear shall make age to be forgotten, or . . . the manifold influences of nature survive during the term of our natural life, so surely my Friend shall forever be my Friend, and reflect a ray of God to me, and time shall foster and adorn and consecrate our friendship, and no less than the ruins of temples. As I love nature, as I love singing birds, and gleaming stubble, and flowing rivers, and morning and evening, and summer and winter, I love thee, my Friend.

Only John could have inspired these words.

In my youth Henry Thoreau was a comrade, Chanticleer crowing atop his roost for the sheer delight of making a noise loud enough to wake his neighbours. Now, thirty years on, as I move rather too briskly through middle age, his song still refreshes my spirit. His thoughts dance like tumblers in a carnival, never failing to raise a broad smile with their muscular, self-conscious agility. *A Week on the Concord and Merrimack Rivers* is a great lusty cry of animality, of a creature stretching itself in every conceivable way, stumbling occasionally, gorging itself at the banquet of life. It is more than a journey of body and mind. It is a testament to the nourishing and healing power of love, friendship and hope.

RICHARD PLATT befriended Henry Thoreau decades ago. (As one would expect, it took time.) Since then, they have ventured forth together with *Ripples from Walden Pond: An Evening with Henry David Thoreau*, a one-man stage presentation. See suggested reading and more at www.RichardPlattAuthor.com.

Decoration by Clare Leighton for an American edition
of Thoreau's *A Week on the Concord and Merrimack Rivers*

# Prayers before Plenty

## ANN KENNEDY SMITH

In 1953 the writer E. M. Forster, then aged 74, was sorting through old family papers and thinking about the past. He had recently moved back to King's College, Cambridge, and the high-ceilinged spacious room where he sat was filled with treasured objects from his previous homes: shelves overflowing with books, framed family portraits on the walls and blue china plates neatly arranged on the mantelpiece. Letters gathered in a drift around his shabby William Morris armchair as he pored over his great-aunt Marianne Thornton's diaries and recollections. She had died when he was 8, but it was thanks to the money she left him that as a young man he was able to study at King's and later to travel to Italy. It was Marianne, more than anyone else, who had helped him to become a writer, and now he wanted to tell her story.

When *Marianne Thornton, 1797–1887: A Domestic Biography* was published three years later, it was greeted as a literary event. It had been five years since the appearance of Forster's *Two Cheers for Democracy*, his collection of critical essays (see *SF* no. 44), and he had not published a novel since *A Passage to India* in 1924. *Marianne Thornton* was widely reviewed, for the most part warmly, although some critics confessed to feeling puzzled by its subject matter. Why, wondered the *Spectator*, did Forster want to cast his considerable charm on the Clapham Sect, that 'particularly uncharming clan'? The

The Abinger edition of E. M. Forster's *Marianne Thornton, 1797–1887: A Domestic Biography* (1956) is available in hardback from André Deutsch: 256pp · £25 · ISBN 9780233993843.

*New York Times* critic admitted that only the writer of *A Passage to India* could have persuaded him to read 'a conversation piece about English family life among the suburban dynasties'.

In the sixty years or so since *Marianne Thornton*'s first publication, it has been leafed through by biographers and scholars rather than read. I think this is a shame, and that this book deserves to be better known. In 2000 it was reissued as part of the Abinger edition, and in her introduction Evelyne Hanquart-Turner describes *Marianne Thornton* as a portrait of a modern Britain in the making, with illuminating glimpses of banking, Parliament and politics, the Church of England and the spread of popular education over nine decades of the nineteenth century. I would add that at a time when British identity is being much discussed, it is a book that seems more relevant than ever.

I discovered it in a King's College archive, where I was working on a book project last summer. It was just before May Week, that confusingly named time in June when the students celebrate after their exams are over, and a marquee was being put up on the front court lawn. The sounds of heavy machinery and men working drifted in through the open window and made it hard to concentrate on handwritten letters, so I took down *Marianne Thornton* from the shelf and began to read. Within minutes I was transported back to another June day in 1806, and a horse-drawn carriage with election ribbons fluttering, going home to Battersea Rise, the house at the heart of this story.

Marianne was born in 1797, the eldest of nine children of Henry Thornton, a wealthy merchant banker and Member of Parliament, and his wife Mary Ann Sykes. Their home was Battersea Rise, an enlarged Queen Anne house on the north-west edge of Clapham Common in south London. The Thorntons belonged to the 'Clapham Sect', a close-knit group of friends that included William Wilberforce, Zachary Macaulay, Granville Sharp and James Stephen, who brought their combined influence, intellect and evangelical zeal to social reform.

Their place of worship was Holy Trinity Church on the Common, presided over by the charismatic Reverend John Venn, and their social centre was Battersea Rise, where lively meetings were held in the oval library with a view of a magnificent tulip tree in the garden.

Battersea Rise was a perfect playground for Marianne and her younger siblings. 'It satisfied in them that longing for a particular place, a home, which is common amongst our upper and middle classes,' Forster observes: 'some of them have transmitted that longing to their descendants, who have lived on into an age when it cannot be gratified.' Writing this in his college rooms, he was thinking of Rooksnest, the cottage in Hertfordshire where he had lived as a child and which he later commemorated in his novel *Howards End*. He had mourned its loss all his life; King's College had provided him with somewhere to live, but it did not feel like home.

From the first pages of the book it is plain that *Marianne Thornton* is as much about Forster as it is about his great-aunt. Threaded through the book are his wry observations, teasing out connections between past and present and poking gentle fun at his illustrious forbears. At times he is combative, reminding us that although the philanthropic Clapham Sect cared passionately about abolishing the slave trade, they were supremely complacent when it came to inequality within their own society. 'When the slavery was industrial they did nothing and had no thought of doing anything.'

But this is a domestic biography, Forster reminds us, and the Thorntons did home life exceedingly well. Adored friends such as William Wilberforce – 'fragile, whimsical, inspired' – and the intellectual 'bishop in petticoats' Hannah More regularly dropped in for dinner. 'Prayers before plenty,' Forster observes, 'But plenty!' Conversations around the table ranged from parliamentary politics to missionary work, from economics to education, and little Marianne was encouraged to take part. Her father taught her about finance and brought her along to his election hustings and George III's opening of Parliament. Despite the constant fear of a French invasion there were long holidays at the seaside, 'comparable with the jauntings of Jane Austen' in their elaborate organization. Fear of Napoleon Bonaparte was the only cloud over this sunny childhood, and Marianne vividly pictured him striding into Battersea Rise and chopping down their beloved tulip tree. Nonsense, her young friend the future historian Thomas Babington Macaulay assured her: when 'Old Boney' came, he would simply stab all the children in their beds.

The world-changing historical events of 1815 were overshadowed for Marianne and her siblings by painful personal loss when both Thornton parents died within the year. Forster skips over the 'superabundance' of long, pious letters from this period and instead describes 19-year-old Marianne's first trip to France, where she and other British tourists flocked after Waterloo. There she fell in love with all things French, and this gave her, Forster is convinced, her Gallic insouciance towards class differences which lasted for the rest of her life.

Her brother Henry, three years younger, was more straitlaced, but brother and sister ran the Thornton family as a team. Together they fought to save the bank where he was a partner when it was hit by a financial crisis in 1825: told through Marianne's recollections, the story is as exciting and dramatic as any novel. Henry coped less well when their younger sister Laura fell in love with a poor Irish clergyman. 'Money must marry money, as it had always done hitherto,' Forster observes drily, and he cheers when, thanks to a particularly spiky letter from a bishop, love wins the day. Laura married the Reverend Charles Forster, and among their ten children brought up in a 'happy insanitary' rectory in Essex was Eddie, the future father of the writer.

Marianne remained unmarried and devoted herself to Battersea Rise and to Henry's three children after he was widowed. The young Forsters often came to visit, and the garden was filled with the sounds of laughter and games. Even sensible Henry occasionally entertained the family with his favourite trick before setting off for work at the bank: after setting fire to a newspaper, he would place it on the seat of his leather armchair then sit down firmly to put the flames out. 'The vision of that substantial extinguisher descending cheers me,' Forster writes: 'the sun comes into the library again, the trees wave freshly on the lawn, tiny cousins collide and jump . . .'

Then Henry fell in love with Emily, his unmarried sister-in-law, and everything changed. Their marriage was not sanctioned under existing British law (the Marriage Act of 1835 made it illegal for a man to marry the sister of his deceased wife) and the ensuing scandal broke the Thornton family apart. The law would remain unchanged until the twentieth century, and writing in Cambridge in the 1950s, when homosexual love was still outlawed in Britain, Forster's anger flashes off the page. It was, he writes, 'yet another example of the cruelty and stupidity of the English Law in matters of sex'. Victorian disapproval did what Bonaparte and the banking crisis had failed to do: it destroyed Battersea Rise.

*Marianne Thornton* immerses us in a lost nineteenth-century world and, as Forster asks, 'Where else could we take such a plunge?' It is an invitation to enjoyment, demonstrating Forster's brilliance as a non-fiction writer and providing us with links to our personal, cultural and national past that otherwise would be lost. Marianne's story unfolds against a rich historical background, from Georgian England to Queen Victoria's Golden Jubilee, in which the Thorntons played an active role.

However, I think that this warm and engaging book is about more than British history and the decline and fall of an influential suburban dynasty. By choosing Marianne as his subject, and telling her story in the way that he does, Forster stresses the importance of personal relations, and the life of the heart and mind rather than public life. He connects his own story to his great-aunt's, and the book's delightful final section is both a memoir of his young life and a love letter to Rooksnest, his childhood home. 'I took it to my heart,' he writes, 'and hoped, as Marianne had of Battersea Rise, that

I should live and die there.' It was not to be, but by writing his great-aunt's story he was able to see that kindness and love were what mattered in the end, and to let go of the past. King's College was his last home, and he was among friends there.

Battersea Rise was swallowed up long ago, and the lawn on which the tulip tree once stood is now covered by houses and streets. Holy Trinity Church still stands on a corner of Clapham Common though, and I went there recently, carrying my copy of *Marianne Thornton*. With its high steeple surrounded by tall, waving trees, the church looks much as it did in the Thorntons' time, and as I approached the imposing portico, the sound of south London traffic seemed to fade away. On an outside wall a stone plaque scarred by Second World War shrapnel commemorates the evangelical and abolitionist work of the Clapham Sect. Then, as I arrive, there is the human touch. A friendly notice on the porch welcomes rough sleepers, and inside a caretaker is boiling a kettle. On a far wall a small brass plaque to Marianne Thornton glints in the shadows.

ANN KENNEDY SMITH lives in Cambridge and is working on her first biography. She is not related to the Kennedy dynasty, so far as she knows.

# Spiritual Reading

ROBIN BLAKE

The school retreat used to be an important annual event in many a Catholic teenager's education. Ours was normally held towards the end of Lent and, though it promised two days of wallowing in my own sinfulness and mortality, it was definitely enjoyable. All lessons were suspended and I welcomed the respite – or blessed relief – from the incessant babble and din of school life, since the retreat was observed in strict silence.

Between the silent meals, stints in church and hard-talking 'discourses' given by a visiting cleric (see Chapter 3 of *A Portrait of the Artist as a Young Man* for these at their most alarming), we spent our time in spiritual reading: simple theology, pious fables, lives of the saints, church history and even fiction, as long as it was on a Catholic theme. Progressing through the school, and growing more (as we thought) sophisticated, we saw it as our duty to try the boundaries of what was acceptable to the Benedictine monks who ruled our lives, and all sorts of arguably Catholic texts were presented for our housemaster Father Brendan's approval. One of my friends was sent packing when he came up with *Brideshead Revisited*, but another was allowed *The Power and the Glory*. Short stories featuring Father Brown and Don Camillo were seen as a lightweight but acceptable choice for a boy on retreat; the Catholic content of Flannery O'Connor's fiction would be dangerously ambiguous and troubling.

Historical novels were well favoured if they told of the persecu-

H. F. M. Prescott, *The Man on a Donkey* (1952)
Apollo Library · Pb · 720pp · £10 · ISBN 9781784977719

tions of the sixteenth and seventeenth centuries, Monsignor Robert Hugh Benson's exemplary *Come Rack! Come Rope!* being a particular favourite. I don't remember anyone proposing *The Fifth Queen*, Ford Madox Ford's fitfully magnificent trilogy of novels about the rise and fall of Katherine Howard, of which the last volume appeared in 1908. Set against the background of the dismantling of Catholicism in England, it is all conspiracy and counter-plot, rush-lit passageways and darkened chambers. Perhaps too political and cynical to have received the housemaster's *nihil obstat*, its plus points would be that Ford draws Henry's penultimate wife – improbably in the eyes of many historians – as an idealist solid for the Old Faith who is pitted against the devious sociopath Thomas Cromwell, herald of self-admiring modernity.

This is the territory now monumentally occupied (though with a very different view of Cromwell) by Hilary Mantel's *Wolf Hall* books. It is also the ground on which stands H. F. M. Prescott's *The Man on a Donkey*, another immense novel that appeared in print roughly midway between the publication of the Ford and Mantel trilogies. This was one Tudor novel the monks were happy to see us reading during the retreat, and it is immediately easy to see why: the story begins in a religious house and, 700 pages later, leaves the reader emotionally in bits following the destruction of that house.

It may seem eccentric to advocate a novel recommended long ago by priests in the same breath as *Come Rack! Come Rope!* But Prescott's book is a very much more formidable and interesting proposition than anything of Mgr Benson's. *The Man on a Donkey* is cast as a chronicle, a form used, as the 'Author's Note' puts it, to introduce the reader into a world where 'he' is at first a stranger but is soon, 'as in real life, picking up, from seemingly trifling episodes, understanding of those about him and learning to know them without knowing what he learns. Only later does the theme of the book emerge.'

That theme is announced by church bells ringing in 1536 across Lincolnshire and Yorkshire, as the common people rise up and muster in huge numbers to perform what they called the Pilgrimage of Grace. It is, in fact, an armed pilgrimage, a rebellion against the religious reforms of Henry VIII and Cromwell, and in particular against their asset-stripping of the monasteries. The novel's underlying theme becomes fully developed at the same time, and it is a moral one – the dictates and betrayals of personal responsibility in human relations, starting with love and family and reaching right up to the acquisitive machinations of the state. The rebellion is, of course, doomed, and as that doom unfolds the novelist's grip tightens, making for a memorable and compelling – and, for many readers, tear-stained – finale.

Prescott's front rank of characters, threaded into the narrative during the period before the rebellion, are Dame Christabel Cowper, a worldly Prioress who will lose her priory; Thomas, Lord Darcy, who will lose his head; Gib Dawe, a priest fanatical for the 'new learning'; Julian, a young girl in love; and the man she loves, lawyer Robert Aske, who will lead the rebellion. At the very start, and here and there throughout, comes the fat, half-crazed, illiterate Yorkshire woman known as Malle, a seer of visions of which 'the man on a donkey' is the main one, though this does seem, when it comes midway through the book, inconsequential and (like all the best visions) elusive of meaning.

Hilda Prescott was a professional historian, and a biographer of Queen Mary Tudor, who knew the sixteenth century like the back of her falconer's glove. She was also a natural novelist who carried out her method of immersing the reader, many pages before the plot takes hold, in the daily life of a long-gone England with astonishing attention to detail. She is careful to count the lapse of time as a Tudor would ('the nearest of the plough teams passed and repassed twice before Julian moved'), she understands the people's daily obsession with fabrics and needlecraft, she tracks and describes the changes in season, weather and land work, she knows that a postern is a side gate, and a sparver is a bed canopy, and much other evocative terminology.

The prose is of its own time, neither prolix in a Victorian way nor modernistically sparse, though it rigorously avoids redundant adjectives and adverbs. Prominence is given to description, and the descriptive passages often have great eloquence, and at times a brio that might be Nabokov: 'the bells began to peal from all the church towers of York, and among them the bells of the Minster, dancing up and down unseen stairways of sound till the air was wild with their flying feet, running after each other, overtaking, clanging together'; or again 'she was young herself and pretty and plump, not heavily plump but with something of the soft airy roundness of a dandelion clock'.

*The Man on a Donkey* gives you its promised thorough immersion in the period but, if you stand back a little, you begin to see how it also resonates with Britain in the 1940s and 1950s when it was conceived, written and published. This is most obvious in the character of Robert Aske. He is just the kind of fellow who tended to crop up in the fiction of the first half of the twentieth century, and in life also. Aske is a romantic hero, certainly, but an accidental one. He is reminiscent of T. E. Lawrence and Richard Hannay and a little, too, of Frodo Baggins, whose adventures were being written up at the same time as Aske's. Both Prescott's sixteenth-century lawyer and Tolkien's intrepid hobbit are 'ordinary' folk who find themselves in a position of leadership that they never sought. Challenged by chance and circumstance to stand up to a force they see as greedy, mechanistic and cruel, they find they cannot resist taking up the cudgels. They also happen to have exactly the degree of cussed determination and simplicity of purpose needed for the job. 'If you hold a thing,' says Aske at one point, 'you sink your teeth into it and grip like a boar hound.'

*The Man on a Donkey*'s romanticism goes deeper than its choice of hero: it is the structural principle of the whole novel. Prescott's view of English history, and in particular of the Reformation, is derived from ideas that had been advanced for a period of more than a century by the likes of Pugin, Wordsworth, Carlyle, William Morris and

G. K. Chesterton. The essence of their argument was that the split with Rome had been the nation's fall from grace, a sort of primal sin in which England turned its face away from the collective and organic life of the Middle Ages and embraced ugly new forms of economic and moral individualism. Adapted by the bestselling Christian socialist historian R. H. Tawney, this idea remained popular well into the twentieth century, and it clearly influenced Prescott. Such thinking was to be overtaken in academia by the anti-romantic pull of modernism and the rigours of structuralist theory, but as a strand of thought it has never quite gone away. Indeed, it re-echoes with renewed persuasiveness now that nature is being duffed up by global warming and humans find themselves more and more manipulated by soulless algorithms.

If this kind of neo-romanticism is encoded in its DNA, the novel's grip is more personal, and this comes from Prescott's richly persuasive prose, and her characters and their predicaments. The reader becomes enmeshed in their fate, in the very needlework of the story, in a way that goes far beyond wanting to know how things will turn out. As I found when I first read it, and again on my recent rereading, *The Man on a Donkey* seemed to demand some sort of commitment from its reader. It challenged me to respond in such a way that I was not simply reading the book, I was also reading *myself* through the book. In a lifetime we are only likely to meet a few texts that can do this and they are, by my reckoning, the best kind of spiritual reading.

ROBIN BLAKE writes mysteries about the eighteenth-century Lancashire coroner Titus Cragg and his friend Dr Luke Fidelis.

# Holding a Mirror

## JOHN CONYNGHAM

Early in 1925 there arrived at the Hogarth Press in London's Tavistock Square a parcel, sent from Zululand, containing the manuscript of *Turbott Wolfe*, the first novel of an unknown writer named William Plomer. Leonard Woolf wrote back promptly, saying it looked 'very interesting' and that once Virginia, who was ill, had read it, he would write again. Plomer, living at a trading store in Entumeni, outside the forested hilltop town of Eshowe (named onomatopoeically in Zulu after the sound of wind in trees), was overjoyed. Two months later, Leonard wrote again, making an offer of publication, and weeks afterwards followed up with the news that Harcourt Brace & Co. in New York wanted to publish it too.

Decades later, while a young sub-editor on *The Natal Witness*, a liberal newspaper in Pietermaritzburg, then something of an English county town transplanted to Africa, I found among the Len Deightons and Wilbur Smiths in a local bookshop a handsome hardback copy of *Turbott Wolfe*, reprinted by the Johannesburg literary publisher Ad Donker and including essays by Roy Campbell, Laurens van der Post and Nadine Gordimer. Being bookish, I wondered why I hadn't heard of the novel, particularly as I had spent my childhood and youth on a sugar-cane farm not far from Entumeni, only to discover that it had long been out of print.

What I then began to read, as Leonard and Virginia Woolf had done half a century earlier, had been written hurriedly by lamplight,

---

William Plomer, *Turbott Wolfe* (1926), is out of print but we can try to obtain second-hand copies.

in hard pencil on thin paper, by a young man barely out of his teens, in his family's wood-and-iron house beside their trading store. Entumeni becomes the fictional Ovuzane, and Zululand Lembuland, where noble Zulus, like the Msomi cousins and the enigmatic maiden Nhliziyombi, are oppressed by settlers with Dickensian names such as Bloodfield and Flesher. Telling the story in the manner of Conrad's Marlow is the eponymous Turbott Wolfe, an artist and former trader, perhaps a genius, who while dying of a fever contracted in Africa lets his mind trawl back over his years in Zululand.

Readers in Britain immediately detected a remarkable new voice, among them Desmond MacCarthy, the literary editor of the *New Statesman*, who became completely engrossed reading it on a train – he later said he hadn't looked out of the window for three hours. American reviewers were similarly admiring, although the *New York World* cautioned, 'Look elsewhere for your bedtime story.'

Many white South Africans, however, were incensed, dismissing Plomer's paean to black dignity and beauty as nasty and pornographic, and the book was kept under lock and key in the Durban Public Library, where it shared a shelf with Rabelais, Boccaccio, *The Origin of Species* and various volumes on classical sculpture. Had Plomer let slip that not only was he racially colour-blind but homosexual too, the baying would have been deafening. Local newspapers and journals hastened to vilify the book, although three reviewers recognized its singular quality. One of the three, gratifyingly to me, was Desmond Young, then editor of *The Natal Witness* which decades later I would join, a Flanders veteran and later an acclaimed biographer of Rommel.

Another of *Turbott Wolfe's* champions was the poet Roy Campbell, the bohemian son of a Durban doctor and member of a prominent sugar-farming family, who had returned home to Natal from London after the triumphant reception of his long poem *The Flaming Terrapin*, and who was shortly to collaborate with Plomer and Laurens van der Post on a short-lived literary magazine, *Voorslag* ('whiplash' in Afrikaans). So energized was Campbell by Plomer's assault on the

smug settler establishment that he celebrated the young novelist in
his satire *The Wayzgoose*:

> Plomer, 'twas you who, though a boy in age,
> Awoke a sleepy continent to rage,
> Who dared alone to thrash a craven race
> And hold a mirror to its dirty face.

Born in 1903 in Pietersburg, a town in the northern Transvaal,
Plomer was technically a South African, but he preferred to see
himself as a 'native' of the country rather than as a full-blown
citizen. Whenever challenged, he would riposte: 'I once had a cat that
had kittens in an oven, but nobody mistook them for cakes.' His
hyphenated Anglo-South African identity was muddied further when
his schooldays at St John's College in Johannesburg were interrupted
by a year-long stint in England at Rugby. Thereafter his father, who
unlike his mother was enamoured of Africa, sent him to a farm with
the Brontë-esque name of Marsh Moor, on the dusty highlands of
the north-eastern Cape, to learn about sheep farming from the Pope
family.

It was during his year with the Popes that the artistic apprentice,
who was clearly unsuited to farming, met several individuals whom
he later, while trading with his parents in Entumeni, turned into
fictional characters. Among these was an itinerant Scottish black-
smith, William Dunbar Macdowall, big-boned and big-hearted and
refreshingly free of racial prejudice, who in *Turbott Wolfe* became the
exemplary Frank d'Elvadere. Others included the Horsehams, an
elderly English-born Anglican priest and his wife in the town of
Molteno, who even in the African heat always had a fire burning in
the grate, and who in conversation contradicted each other comically;
they, together with their quirks, became the Fotheringhays. Marsh
Moor's owner, Fred Pope, a conservative Anglophile with whom
Plomer had a complicated though mutually respectful relationship,

appears as Soper, a farmer heartily disliked in the Ovuzane district because he is more industrious and successful than his neighbours.

Combine all these characters in a colonial setting and you have the plot of *Turbott Wolfe*, which is essentially a shadow play of Plomer's experiences in rural Zululand. Towards the end of the story, various Africans and settlers, seeking a more equitable society, form an association named Young Africa, but it comes to nothing. If all this sounds thin, and if *Turbott Wolfe* does have its immaturities, Plomer's clean, clear prose has an exhilarating energy. From the very start, like MacCarthy I was spellbound by the masterful writing, even if the master was barely 20 years old.

Years later, while puzzling over the impact of *Turbott Wolfe*, Laurens van der Post recalled from his youth that when captured baboons were handed mirrors, each became convinced that the image confronting it was another baboon rather than a reflection of itself. Agitatedly peering behind the mirror, each sought the threatening 'other' and, on repeatedly finding nothing, grew vengeful and smashed its mirror into pieces. Such behaviour, van der Post realized, explained *Turbott Wolfe*'s stormy reception in South Africa. Indeed, why else in the story would white farmers who themselves had black concubines be so righteously incensed when Mabel van der Horst, a strapping settler Amazon in the mould of Joan Hunter Dunn, determinedly marries the man she loves, the Zulu intellectual Zachary Msomi?

Worn down by life, Turbott Wolfe announces that he is going to sell his trading store and leave Zululand. When his assistant Caleb asks him what he plans to do next, he replies: 'I have just enough money to go and live quietly in England. I shall live in London. I shall dress neatly and inconspicuously, but with distinction.' And that of course is what Plomer himself would eventually do.

First, though, he moved to Sezela, on the coast south of Durban, where he collaborated with Campbell and van der Post on *Voorslag*. Then he caught a ship to Japan where on Campbell's recommend-

© National Portrait Gallery

ation Edmund Blunden, then visiting Professor of English at Tokyo's Imperial University, found him a job as an English tutor. Plomer settled eventually in London, as he had predicted, becoming a reader at Jonathan Cape and a linchpin of the literary establishment, and counting among his friends the Woolfs, Elizabeth Bowen, E. M. Forster and W. H. Auden.

Determined never to write for money or to follow fashion, over the years Plomer quietly accumulated a distinguished corpus of novels, poems, short stories, librettos, biographies and volumes of autobiography, each characteristically elegantly crafted. He also edited the diaries of Francis Kilvert, bringing a forgotten Victorian clergyman vividly back to life.

Among the submissions crossing his desk at Jonathan Cape, Plomer also 'discovered' the poet Derek Walcott, later a Nobel laureate, and ushered into print the then unknown writers Arthur Koestler, Alan Paton, Stevie Smith and John Fowles. And when the manuscript of *Under the Volcano*, sent by Malcolm Lowry, then living in a squatter shack in Dollarton, British Columbia, reached Cape's London offices, it was Plomer's meticulous response that prompted Lowry's lengthy validation, itself a literary curiosity. But Plomer's most notable act of literary midwifery, in the public's eyes at least, was bringing James Bond into the world.

Years earlier, having read *Turbott Wolfe* while a schoolboy at Eton, Ian Fleming had sent Plomer a fan letter, and during the Second World War they worked together in Naval Intelligence. Unsure of his writing ability, Fleming distrusted intellectuals but felt immediately at ease with the courteous and considerate Plomer. So when, in 1951 at 'Goldeneye', his holiday home in Jamaica, Fleming wrote a thriller, it was to his friend that he tentatively presented it. Plomer knew at once that it was a sure-fire money-spinner but had difficulty convincing his colleagues. Disliking thrillers, Jonathan Cape himself had to be persuaded to read it, but eventually *Casino Royale* was born. Jonathan Cape the company became the Bond books' publisher, even if its co-founder and namesake never read another one of them. In thanks, Fleming dedicated *Goldfinger* 'To my gentle Reader William Plomer'.

JOHN CONYNGHAM was for decades a journalist, chasing his tail on a daily newspaper. With three novels and a sugar-farm memoir under his belt, at his home outside Pietermaritzburg he is now working on another novel.

# Man on the Run

DEREK COLLETT

I have a good public character and a respectable position in society. I live by myself, and for years past have given no one any account of my movements; I am quick-witted and ready for nearly anything; I think I have little personal or social conscience. Above all, I am a murderer . . .

The voice is that of Desmond Thane, hero of John Mair's only novel and one of the most extravagantly larger-than-life fictional characters I have ever come across. Though he displays an unappealing mixture of some of the worst human characteristics – vanity, arrogance, self-centredness, cowardice and mendacity to name but a few – Mair succeeds in making Desmond intensely likeable, and one can't help rooting for him and hoping he will survive each fresh predicament that confronts him.

In 1990, I watched a drama series on the BBC called *Never Come Back*. It was a superb Second World War thriller with a fine cast including James Fox, Nathaniel Parker and Martin Clunes. Then about a year later, while browsing in my local bookshop, I pulled a volume entitled *Never Come Back* by John Mair off the shelf and realized that the television series must have been an adaptation of it. The book had obviously been on display in the shop window for a long time because its front cover was badly faded. I almost put it back on the shelf. Thank goodness I didn't, because *Never Come Back* (1941) has since become one of my favourite novels.

John Mair, *Never Come Back* (1941), is out of print but we can obtain second-hand copies.

I find it difficult to put into words exactly what it was that captivated me when I first read it all those years ago, but I do remember experiencing a delicious shiver of anticipation as I read the opening lines. Some writers are like that: you just feel very comfortable with them right from the start and sense that, in their hands, satisfaction is virtually guaranteed. So it was with me and John Mair.

I have reread *Never Come Back* many times since and always find something new in it. Like *The Small Back Room* by Nigel Balchin and *The Ordeal of Gilbert Pinfold* by Evelyn Waugh, it is one of my 'desert island' books, one I tend to return to when I'm feeling low and in need of a literary pick-me-up, and it never fails.

Set in London during the Phoney War, *Never Come Back* opens with the account of an unsatisfactory romantic liaison between Desmond, a journalist, and the cold, dark and mysterious Anna Raven. Desmond picks Anna up in the Café Royal, is initially intrigued by her and quickly becomes besotted. To his fury, though, Anna does not fully reciprocate his advances, so he arranges a meeting at her flat. This culminates in a violent quarrel when he attempts to read her diary; there is a struggle, and Desmond strangles Anna. Though frightened at the thought of what might happen to him now, Desmond is far from contrite: 'He felt no sort of conscience or pity for Anna . . . death had killed his interest in her.' So he pockets Anna's diary and removes himself from the scene.

Three days later Desmond is apprehended by two men who tell him they are police officers. They bundle him into a car and drive him to a large, isolated house in Hertfordshire. Here Desmond is detained for several days before being alternately questioned by a man named Foster and tortured by his two accomplice kidnappers. Needless to say, they have nothing to do with the Metropolitan Police. Foster is a representative of 'The International Opposition', an organization described as being 'a Federal Union of the dispossessed' who 'represent all the great ideological minorities of Europe' currently out of power. The aim of the IO is to bring about 'simultaneous coups in all the capitals that shall give us power – and revenge – in our separate countries'.

Anna, it turns out, was an IO agent and her diary is actually a 'Contact List' – a coded notebook containing details of British members of IO. To the IO committee its loss is an emergency, and its recovery of the utmost importance. Threaded through the narrative, the deliberations of this committee as they oversee the hunt for the Contact List are some of the most entertaining committee meeting minutes one is ever likely to read.

Helped by his ignorance of the true nature of the diary and unaware that Anna was a spy, Desmond holds out under torture. Then, by showing a light in his cell during the blackout, he succeeds in attracting the attention of the local bobby. When the policeman knocks on the front door, Desmond manages to make his escape.

What follows, as he is pursued across southern England by Foster and his cohorts, is a sort of compendium of well-worn thriller scenarios. There is a gunfight among some railway trucks; an exciting moonlit chase on foot; a cold-blooded murder; experiments in code-breaking; a phoney doctor; and some slow-witted heavies. But despite the familiarity of the components there is nothing stale or second-hand in the telling, which creates an atmosphere of suspicion and paranoia.

In his introduction to one edition of the novel, the crime writer Julian Symons observed that Mair 'had obviously read Eric Ambler, who seems responsible for a touch here or there'. Desmond certainly has a good deal in common with the protagonists of early man-on-the-run Ambler thrillers such as *Uncommon Danger* and *Journey into Fear*: innocent professional men who find themselves caught up in life-threatening political machinations. Admittedly Desmond cannot be described as 'innocent', but the rest of the comparison rings true. And there are echoes too of novels like *The Thirty-Nine Steps*, early Graham Greene 'entertainments' such as *A Gun for Sale* and Geoffrey Household's classic novel of pursuit *Rogue Male*, which was published just a year before Mair began writing *Never Come Back*.

The pace does slacken somewhat about two-thirds of the way through, but the story gains fresh momentum when Foster recaptures his escaped prisoner. As a reward for disclosing the whereabouts of the Contact List, Desmond is sentenced to death – but of course I'm not about to reveal what happens next. I will only say that the ingenious and unexpected ending is at once believable and chilling.

John Mair has been so utterly forgotten since his early death in 1942 that he doesn't even have his own Wikipedia page, let alone an entry in the *Oxford Dictionary of National Biography*. He was born in 1913, attended Westminster School and University College, London, and then became a literary journalist, reviewing books for periodicals including the *New Statesman* and working part-time for *John o' London's Weekly*. He was a gambler, something of a dandy and an engaging conversationalist – as indeed is Desmond Thane, who is to some extent a self-portrait. Called up in the early stages of the Second World War, Mair joined the RAF as a Pilot Officer and was killed in a plane crash off the Yorkshire coast before he had turned 30. He wrote one other book, *The Fourth Forger* (1938), but *Never Come Back* is his great achievement.

So what makes the novel so special, and why does it still deserve to be read, more than three-quarters of a century after it was first published? Well, it turns some earlier thriller conventions on their heads – particularly in its introduction of an amoral anti-hero – and it is written with tremendous self-confidence and brio. *Never Come Back* is a wonderful mélange of thrills, comedy, wartime atmosphere and sparkling dialogue, and if you have not read it I would urge you to do so at the earliest opportunity. I don't think you will regret it.

DEREK COLLETT is a scientific editor and proofreader, an occasional writer of magazine articles, a devotee of 1940s novels and the author of *His Own Executioner: The Life of Nigel Balchin*.

# Melancholy but Marvellous

ARIANE BANKES

The capital of nowhere – could anywhere be more tantalizing? For those of us increasingly blasé or wary about visiting 'somewheres' the world over, many of them the target of hordes of other tourists hell-bent on pleasure (and often compromising the particular qualities of their destination in the process), nowhere sounds the ultimate place to go. And, as it turns out, this place does have its own geographical co-ordinates, and is even accessible by public transport. It's just that on arrival you may experience a sudden sense of dislocation, an overwhelming wistfulness for an elusive past, and a present that feels curiously like limbo. For in the words of its chronicler, Jan Morris, in *Trieste and the Meaning of Nowhere* (2001), the Mediterranean port 'stands above economics, or tourism, or science, or even the passage of ships, or if not above them, apart from them'. And it is a city whose precarious geographical position and contested imperial history have, she thinks, bred a civility rare in our hectic times, a simple decency that makes the place a 'half-real, half-wishful Utopia'. That was certainly our experience on a recent visit; we were tactfully absorbed into the gentle mêlée of city life, and warmly welcomed into the quirky museums and houses that keep the city's complex history alive.

It is hardly surprising to discover that Morris's elegiac meditation on Trieste, published at the turn of the century after a lifetime of acquaintance with the place, stands as her own favourite among all her many works, and that Trieste was the model for her imaginary

---

Jan Morris, *Trieste and the Meaning of Nowhere* (2001)
Faber · Pb · 208pp · £9.99 · ISBN 9780571204687

'favourite' city of Hav. *Trieste and the Meaning of Nowhere* was to have been her swansong, which adds a layer of poignancy to any reading (in fact, she has since brought out a delightful short tribute to Vittore Carpaccio, that most irresistible of Venetian artists). Her affection for the place is so contagious that I was immediately seduced on a first reading, and felt I was being re-introduced to a forgotten but once familiar friend, despite having no Austro-Hungarian antecedents and little knowledge of Mitteleuropa. I was soon on a train from Venice, her book in hand.

Although Morris never tells you how to find such-and-such a square or when that favourite watering hole is open for business, I felt the need for no other guide. For she conjures up such a rich experience of the city, past and present, that it enfolds you like a cloak, and propels you through streets and squares alive with ghosts and charged with layers of history.

Appropriately, the book begins in a haze of uncertainty and deprecation:

> I cannot always see Trieste in my mind's eye. Who can? It is not one of your iconic cities, instantly visible in the memory or the imagination. It offers no unforgettable landmark, no universally familiar melody, no unmistakable cuisine, hardly a single native name that everyone knows.

How different from Morris's paean to Venice, written forty years earlier (when Jan was still James), which is muscular, almost baroque in comparison. That city, too, was liminal: 'half eastern, half western, half land, half sea, poised between Rome and Byzantium, between Christianity and Islam, one foot in Europe, the other paddling in the pearls of Asia'. It was surely that very quality of ambiguity that so captured Morris's imagination at that particular point in his life.

It was as a young army subaltern that James first visited both cities in 1946, en route for Palestine, and it was Venice that lingered then in his memory, its deserted squares and crumbling palaces 'clothed always . . . in a pale green light' and beckoning return. Trieste on the other hand inspired, even in a 19-year-old, a 'maudlin essay' on the subject of nostalgia, written in a dog-eared notebook and since mislaid. It now seems curiously prescient, for then 'I pined for a Europe that seemed in my fancy to form a cohesive whole, sharing values and manners and aspirations, and when I looked around me at the Trieste of 1946, I thought I could see the ghost of that ideal.' However mistaken that notion turned out to be, Morris has returned to her capital of nowhere at regular intervals, exploring its topography, conjuring up inhabitants past and present, and trying to nail its essence, an essence so elusive that even she cannot entirely pin it down.

In doing so she doesn't romanticize the city; she is brisk about its shortcomings: its 'damned monotonous summer', in the words of James Joyce who spent fifteen indigent but creative years there, writing most of *Ulysses*; its roiling *bora*, the ferocious wind from the *Karst* that scours its streets and scatters its citizens in disarray; its brooding sea and 'weeping' castle of Miramar.

Built atop a promontory overlooking the city by the idealistic young Maximilian, younger brother of the Hapsburg Emperor, and intended as a love nest for his Belgian bride, Carlotta, the castle was abandoned when he sailed for Mexico, there to meet his death at the hands of a firing squad (so shockingly imagined by Edouard Manet). Ever since, this landmark has been so haunted by gloom that all who have lived there seem to have come to a sorry end, some (like the unfortunate Carlotta) going mad along the way. With its elaborate white towers and crenellations, it shines like a beacon through sun and sea mist on the horizon; close to, it looms over its precipice in the golden Mediterranean light like a fantasy by Claude Lorrain.

As Vienna's grand seaport, a pivot between Europe and Asia, Trieste enjoyed its golden age in the nineteenth century. It was the quintessential melting-pot, containing half the peoples of Europe, who spoke in as many languages: Latins, Slavs, Greek ship-owners, English aesthetes, German barons, Marxist adventurers – all found a berth there. Money was the lure. Newly enriched merchants held sway, and mercantile and civic buildings shot up, each more extravagant than the last. Protocol and frequent parades were the order of the day, the latter believed by the Emperor Franz Josef to be the best way to tame dissent.

But this era of pomp and not a little pretension did not last. With the Risorgimento gaining ground, Garibaldi's Italian nationalists were soon at the city's gates. This once complacent Austrian satellite became a hotbed of revolutionary fervour, a seething swamp of irredentists hanging out in the Caffè San Marco and fomenting bloodshed. Subterfuge was rife, explosives were ubiquitous; according to the Victorian writer and traveller Isabel Burton, if Austrians gave a party, Italians would throw a bomb into it, and members of the Imperial family visiting from Vienna were greeted with 'a chorus of bombs, bombs on the railway, bombs in the garden, bombs in the sausages'. A statue of Verdi (whose very name was an acronym for Italian nationalism, standing for Vittorio Emanuele Re d'Italia) was erected to cock a snook at the Austrians, and Franz Josef, taking the hint, sorrowfully gave Trieste a wide berth thereafter.

Nevertheless it was to Trieste that the corpses of his nephew, Archduke Franz Ferdinand, and his wife Sophie were brought by battleship following their assassination at Sarajevo, en route for Vienna. The shock of their funeral procession, its stiff formality caught by a local cameraman, distilled the trauma of a continent and foretold the end of an empire. With memories like these, Morris observes, 'melancholy is Trieste's chief rapture'. But never once does her book lower the spirits; instead, it serves as an intriguing and upbeat exploration of the very nature of melancholy.

For Morris, the city is an allegory not just of limbo but of life, and she sees her own reflected in its changing fortunes: 'After a lifetime of describing the planet, I look at Trieste now as I would look in a mirror,' she writes from the vantage point of her declining years.

Wedged between the sea and the looming *Karst*, Trieste is still a cosmopolitan city but one without a hinterland, let alone an empire. Unhooked from its imperial past, its heyday was brief: after a bright blast of celebration at gaining its freedom in 1918, and a few months in the public gaze as the launch pad for Gabriele d'Annunzio's extravagant raid on nearby Fiume, it sank back into its habitual torpor. Its streets and squares bear grandiose Italian names that date from decades of unopposed nationalism, shading into sycophantic fascism during Mussolini's sway. When he paid a lightning visit in 1938, 'uniformed functionaries by the thousand, formidable or ridiculous, fat or weedy, paraded here and there in jackboots and tasselled hats, swelling out their chests'. But by then the city had become essentially a backwater, and for all the braggadocio of this brief episode, so it has remained: Italian in name but fundamentally amorphous and unaligned in nature.

It has also lost its principal *raison d'être*, and how can it make up for that? 'If it were not a port Trieste would have been nothing much,' writes Morris, 'and the sense that it is nothing much, now that its great days seem to be gone, is what has made it feel so wistfully unfulfilled.' So if you are experiencing a little wistful unfulfilment, 'a fragrant sense of might-have-been' in these stark post-referendum times, there can be nowhere more in tune with your mood. Book your passage now.

ARIANE BANKES is the author of a monograph and co-curator of an exhibition about David Jones. She would like to revisit Trieste at regular intervals, each visit bringing a deeper unravelling of its resonant past.

# Hair Today and Gone Tomorrow

ANDY MERRILLS

Five or six summers ago, I was browsing in a shabbily genteel second-hand bookstore in a university town somewhere in the middle of the United States. The shop had a substantial stock of fiction, a generous and eclectic supply of non-fiction and the sort of haphazard shelving policy which actively demands exploration. I cannot now remember which section I was in when I discovered Reginald Reynolds's extraordinary *Beards: An Omnium Gatherum* (1949). I'm pretty sure it wasn't in fiction, but beyond that it could have been anywhere. The British Library shelves the book under 'hairstyles'; the Library of Congress under 'fashion'; Cambridge University Library under 'European History'. The seller's pencilling on the fly-leaf simply reads 'History (?)', which is probably where it was. But the uncertainty speaks volumes.

It was the cover that first drew my attention – the title on the paperback edition sprouts wildly across the chin of a figure who looks rather like Karl Marx – but it was the preface that ensured I bought the book. As part of his rambling discussion of the book's genesis, Reynolds turns to the subject of serendipity, and the discovery of unexpected delights while browsing:

> Now any good library is to a Serendipitist what a fly-paper is to a fly; and the most dangerous of all such fly-papers to a fly of small learning, such as myself, is the Reading Room of the British Museum. You ask for some old pamphlet or broadsheet,

---

Reginald Reynolds, *Beards: An Omnium Gatherum* (1949), is out of print but we can obtain second-hand copies.

and it is certain to arrive in a bound volume with some twenty
others or more, that are all the more entertaining because they
have nothing in common with your studies. Or again, you are
reading a life of Pomponius Atticus, who does not interest you,
when you find that he died of *tenesmos*, which lays a hold of
your curiosity. A considerate footnote explains that this afflic-
tion is *a Violent Motion without the Power of going to Stool*; and
a new word with a sinister sound and truly terrifying connota-
tion is added to your vocabulary. It will explain almost any
modern poet, except Mr Betjeman, and can be swung on the
head of any adverse critic of this book who has not himself
written a volume on beards.

Fellow enthusiasts of Reynolds's *Beards* occasionally surface online
and more rarely in person. Almost invariably, their first encounters
with the book and its author prove to have been remarkably similar
to my own – a chance find in a bookshop, a choked-off laugh of
confusion at the cover (the dust jacket and endpapers of the 1949
Allen & Unwin hardback are even better), and then sheer delight at
those opening words.

The book itself is a genuinely extraordinary mixture of the
whimsical, the esoteric and the intimidatingly learned. Reynolds observes for example that beards typically become most
prominent during periods of rule by strong women – a point
he illustrates with reference to the pointed barbs of Elizabethan
courtiers in the portraits at the National Gallery, and to the
bushes that festooned the chins of 'muscular' Christian missionaries
during Victoria's reign. He presents this as an assertion of unambiguous
masculinity during a period when gender roles seemed to be in flux (at
least to the beard-growers), and this seems plausible enough. But reading *Beards* simply as a great treasure trove of information and
observation misses the joy at the heart of the book. This is the work of
a (clean-shaven) author who delights in the impossible scale of his task.

The point comes across rather well in the substantial appendices that follow the text proper (many of them excellent small essays in their own right): Bearded Women; The Capuchin Beard; Czar Nicholas I and the Beard; Dedication of Hair; Pogonology; Saxon Beards; Sunday Shaving; The Beard of Jonas; and Women and Beards (Male). As the headings suggest, these are presented with a light heart, but the relentlessness of the parade of learning is quite dizzying.

When I'm not browsing in bookshops, I teach and conduct research in ancient and medieval history. As it happens, beards were quite important in the period that I know best. The emperor Marcus Aurelius was proud of his philosopher's beard. Julian the Apostate – the quixotic philosopher-warrior of the fourth century who lasted just two frenzied years on the imperial throne before being killed trying to conquer Persia in emulation of Alexander the Great – was so pleased with his (and so proud of his rhetorical sophistry) that he composed a bizarre treatise entitled *Misopogon* ('Beard-hater') as a self-satire. This caused much confusion among his clean-shaven critics, who objected less to his hairstyle than to his attempts to restore paganism to an increasingly Christian world, and who never seem to have appreciated his eccentric sense of humour.

I should also add that one of the many barbarian groups who carved up the western Roman empire in what we used to call the 'Dark Ages' took their very name from their exuberant facial furniture: the Langobards (or 'Long-beards') even circulated myths which traced their origins and their name to the wearing of false beards before their gods. This is the kind of stuff that you pick up around the edges of an academic career – when idly wondering if there might be an article in ancient beards, and then deciding there probably isn't. Reynolds includes it all. His research for the book must have been prodigious, and he must have been a sensational dinner-party companion. Incidentally, Pomponius Atticus (a philosopher and correspondent of Cicero's) may also have had a beard, which would explain what Reynolds was looking for that day in the British Library.

*Beards* was prescient. A quick Internet search reveals a considerable sprouting of beard-themed books over the last decade or so: *One Thousand Beards: A Cultural History of Facial Hair* (2002); *The World Beard and Moustache Championships* (2004); *Beards: A Spotter's Guide* (2010); *The Little Book of Beards* (2014); *The Philosophy of Beards* (2014). At the very least, then, we could present Reynolds's self-styled *Omnium Gatherum* as classic loo-reading *avant la lettre*. Or we could if Reynolds hadn't beaten us to it. Six years before the publication of *Beards*, in 1943, Reynolds finished his magisterial *Cleanliness and Godliness* – a similarly exhaustive cultural history of the loo, which is every bit as delightful and peculiar as its successor. There is too a delicious irony in the fact that *Cleanliness* was published at the height of the war, when there was a major paper shortage in London.

It's worth pointing out at this stage that neither *Cleanliness* nor *Beards* is a straightforwardly comic work. Much of their delight comes from the relentless presentation of esoterica. By taking himself seriously as a pogonologist and balneologist, Reynolds created works that are both infinitely richer and much funnier than the profusion of disposable books that have been written on similar topics in recent years. In the end, both are about precisely that serendipity that Reynolds celebrates in the opening of *Beards* – the delights to be found in the library, and the unexpected connections that can be made even with the least promising material. Within these works, Reynolds champions the trivial – and that is no small feat.

The greater irony is perhaps that Reginald Reynolds is remembered (if at all) as a purveyor of fine trivia rather than as the astute political commentator that he was. Reynolds was a Quaker, a committed pacifist and a life-long opponent of imperialism. Before the Second World War, he travelled across much of the British Empire and wrote a great deal about it. The best known of his pre-war writing focused on India, and sought to explain Gandhi's independence movement to a largely hostile (and generally ignorant) British public. His essays on Gandhi's hunger strikes, and the broad polemic *White Sahibs in India* (1937) are not in the least funny, but then nor were the causes that Reynolds sought to explain. Instead, they are concerned with the fundamental injustice of British imperialism, and they make the point vividly and persuasively. It is perhaps no surprise that Nehru wrote the preface for *White Sahibs*.

Reynolds's post-war writing also focused upon the comparable issues raised by the British presence in Africa. His *Beware of Africans* (1955) draws on his travels through the continent, and again makes an exceptionally persuasive case for rolling up the old map of empire.

There is much more to be said about Reginald Reynolds. He was married to the novelist, philosopher and activist Ethel Mannin, and Robert Huxter's fine biography *Reg and Ethel* (1993) provides a wonderful introduction to them both. His was a life lived against the grain, and nowhere is this more evident than in his marvellous book on beards.

ANDY MERRILLS lives and works in the East Midlands, when he isn't poking around bookshops throughout the world. He wears a beard.

---

## Coming attractions

MARGARET DRABBLE sees Ireland through Trollope's eyes · MICHAEL LEAPMAN meets a well-tempered gardener · DAISY HAY is compelled by the London of Barnaby Rudge · ANTHONY GARDNER shares Osbert Lancaster's Edwardian childhood · MARTIN SORRELL sits out the plague year in Oran · JUSTIN MAROZZI travels dangerously with Rosita Forbes · HELENA DRYSDALE skips school and takes to the woods · ANDREW NIXON explores an acute case of topophilia

# Bibliography

### *Blowing Our Own Trumpet!*

'Dear Slightly Foxed, A short while ago I made the very bad decision to cancel my subscription to *SF*. Now I find that I simply can't do without it. Would it be possible to start it again from when it stopped, so I don't lose any issues? Yours in hope'
B. Champness, Cornwall

'This is to let you know that I have just received the latest *SF*, for which many thanks. Once again a breath of civilization, culture, good humour and intelligence has entered my life.'
G. Grayston, Australia

'Slightly Foxed, I have received your beautiful little books! They are such a pleasure to read, and even to just look at and hold. Thanks for the handwritten note, I appreciate your attention to detail and quality!'
W. Carriger, United States

'Dear Slightly Foxed, The latest edition arrived in Anguilla last week, as we were trying to clean up after a direct hit from Hurricane Irma. It gave me wonderful relief from the stress for a couple of hours. Thank you'
M. Mitchell, Anguilla

'Hi Hattie, Thanks so much for your response. I ordered the Carey volume and submitted payment just now for it. Thank you again for having such a wonderful business and creating such lovely books for us all! Warmly'
N. Sheeley, Canada